Shall We Dance?

An Enlightened Spiritual Approach to Becoming Jewish by Choice

Maggidah Shoshannah Brombacher, PhD
&
Rabbi Bruce D. Forman, PhD

2021

TotalRecall Publications, Inc.
1103 Middlecreek
Friendswood, Texas 77546
281-992-3131 281-482-5390 Fax
www.TotalRecallPress.com

All rights reserved. Except as permitted under the United States Copyright Act of 1976, No part of this publication may be reproduced, stored in a retrieval system, or transmitted in any form or by any means electronic or mechanical or by photocopying, recording, or otherwise without prior permission of the publisher. Exclusive worldwide content publication / distribution by TotalRecall Publications, Inc.

Copyright © 2021 by: Shoshannah Brombacher, Ph.D.
And Bruce D. Forman, Ph.D.
Cover design by: Shoshannah Brombacher
All rights reserved
ISBN: 978-1-64883-108-9
UPC: 6-43977-41089-4

Library of Congress Control Number: 2021941560

FIRST EDITION
1 2 3 4 5 6 7 8 9 10

The scanning, uploading and distribution of this book via the Internet or via any other means without the permission of the publisher is illegal and punishable by law. Please purchase only authorized electronic editions, and do not participate in or encourage electronic piracy of copyrighted materials. Your support of the author's rights is appreciated.

We want to express our thanks to Matt Hedrick and Amanda Strunin for their editorial comments on an earlier draft of this manuscript.

This book is dedicated to Rabbi Bruce's rebbe, Rabbi Joseph Gelberman (z'tl), and to Maggidah Shoshannah's friends who uncovered their Jewish souls and joined the Tribe.

What others say about this book:

Books on Jewish conversion line the shelves of many libraries and bookstores.
Why another? A major reason is the approach to the topic, an approach which is multi-dimensional and non-judgmental. This is indeed reflected in examples given in the work where opposing opinions and viewpoints are offered by each author. Added to this is the emphasis on the concept and the progression of the conversion process rather than details and minutiae of a specific movement's requirements. Lastly, there are topics more often than not unseen in other books of this nature, e.g., beards, tattoos, x-mas trees.
All in all, this is an important go-to book for a fresh and clear approach to an oftentimes complex subject.

Rabbi Steven J. Kaplan, PhD, Dean Judaic Institute for Graduate Studies

I have been a practicing Jew all my life. I was still able to learn a great deal from the 50 questions posed by the authors. If that were not enough, the art work was magnificent and truly enhanced each section. This book is totally appropriate for anyone who truly wants a deeper understanding of the Jewish faith.

Robert Gropper, PhD Associate Professor Emeritus at the University of Miami

Through unique storytelling and insightful answers to 50 timeless questions, this book makes learning complex Jewish values and Judaism easy and fun for readers of all ages. A delightful guide, full of inspiration and information for those who wish to learn and become authentically Jewish by choice in the modern world.

Weidong Xia, Ph.D., Professor and Knight-Ridder Center Research Fellow Florida International University

The authors address important questions about Judaism that are not typically considered in traditional conversion classes. They simplify complex issues in a forthright and balanced manner and sprinkle the discussion with entertaining stories. And, the artwork is captivating. I now have another valuable resource to recommend to all of my conversion students.

Rabbi/Cantor Gregory Groysman, Director Rabbinical Services Center of America

Shall We Dance? An Enlightened Spiritual Approach to Becoming Jewish by Choice provides important insights into the nature of Judaism and what it means to be Jewish. So many offerings on such subjects are dry, dense, and unapproachable. The work of Brombacher and Forman has been broken down into bite-size capsules that are easy to digest, pleasant to the palate, and filling to the spirit. Read this volume in one sitting or read it in 50 doses over the course of a year or two. It's well worth the read!

Rabbi Merrill Shapiro, President Saint Augustine Jewish Historical Society

bs"d

Preface

Albert Einstein once said he wished he was not born Jewish.
In this way he could choose Judaism.

Echoing the sentiments of Protestants Thomas Jefferson and James Madison, in 1965 the Roman Catholic Church's Second Vatican Council produced a document known as *Dignitatus Humanae*, a universal declaration on human rights. This document emphasized the right of every human being to express the spiritual side of her/his nature by having the freedom to choose any avenue of religious practice s/he may find suitable. There is a long tradition in human history where the rights of others have been denied, or denigrated, and it was time to right this wrong. Whether it is by forced conversion at the hands of militant violent actors, missionary zeal, or the subtle expression of anti-Muslim or antisemitic attitudes, the result is a dehumanizing abridgment of the fundamental human right of religious freedom. Unfortunately, violation of this basic human right continues with alarming regularity in Africa, Asia, the Middle East, and other parts of the world. And also, here in the United States.

Respect for human dignity, kindness to others, pursuit of social justice, and caring for the environment are values found in Judaism dating back thousands of years. Certainly, at the time Judaism was born it was the first and—for a long time—the only truly ethical religion, with well-regulated rights for slaves and animals, in especially for ancient times unique and humane ways. In our time, we agree that no one should be a slave, but at a time when most people considered slaves as chattel, treating them like thinking and feeling human beings with a chance to be set free was a large leap forward in the evolution of human thinking. Consider, for instance, the treatment of a female prisoner of war in Deuteronomy 23:1-13. She is allowed to mourn her parents (and other relatives killed in the war) for a whole month. Only after that month has passed the man who captured her should marry her, not just use her as a sex slave. But when he grows tired of her he cannot simply send her away. She is his wife. How different is this treatment from the fate of the sex slaves taken by ISIS in our time? Add to that our rich history of ideas and culture, and we may get a glimpse into why Judaism can be an attractive path to spiritual fulfillment.

A courtship dance is seen among many species and some human societies. Notably, it is absent among Jews. For Orthodox Jews, a woman touching a man is not permitted except among married couples, and then there are many rules governing when touching is permissible. Of course, touching children and (grand)parents is acceptable, but we mean a man and a woman here in a romantic, sexual context. We dance, but we dance at the wedding. Not before. We've chosen this term for our title because we want to emphasize that when someone is considering conversion to Judaism, it is similar to the dance that is performed during a period of attraction, followed by growing mutual interactions that may culminate in a match. We also want to emphasize through this metaphor that in our view, which is outside of the mainstream, traditions and rituals should not be accepted uncritically. Instead they should be considered thoughtfully, questioned, and adapted to one's lifestyle in ways that are personally meaningful. And finally, just like we refrain from dancing before a wedding, Judaism does not look for converts. Those who are interested in Judaism must take the initiative and step forward. They start with learning what Judaism is about.

In this book, we pose 50 significant questions about Judaism. Some may appear to be more relevant to you than others. We chose this number because it represents the Fifty Gates of Understanding our Sages talked about in ancient writings. We pose questions, because in our tradition dialogue and query have been considered essential, not only to be engaged in a process to achieve knowledge and insight, but more importantly, to engender an inquisitive approach and desire to pursue lifelong learning. This is an important Jewish value. The Haggadah tells us the Passover story, and opens with the words *Tzei ulemad*, go out and learn. That is the essence of Judaism! Not only should we learn and study, we should also look at every question from more than one perspective. The Torah is traditionally studied in four different ways, a method called *PaRDeS*, which is an acronym of:
- *Peshat*, which is the literal meaning of a text,
- *Remez*, explaining a verse in the text by relating to other texts,
- *Derash*, explaining the meaning of a verse with the help of homiletics, parables, and the like, and
- *Sod,* the mystical, secret meaning. In Hebrew, the word *pardes* means garden, or paradise.

So, you see, Judaism is a garden with so many different plants and flowers, that you won't live long enough to see, smell and taste all of them. To illustrate this perspective on questions we want to tell you a story.

A man goes to his rabbi, says he wants to learn Talmud, and become wise like our sages. "All right," says the rabbi, "we'll start with some questions. Two men fall down a chimney. One comes out dirty and the other comes out clean. Which one washes?"

The man ponders the question and says, "The dirty one washes."

"Good," replies the rabbi, "now, in another scenario two men fall down a chimney. One comes out dirty and the other comes out clean. Which one washes?"

"Didn't I just answer that?" asks the man.

The rabbi says, "No, this is a different question."

The man replies "The dirty one."

"No" says the rabbi, "The dirty one sees that his companion is clean, and thinks he is also clean, so he does not wash. On the other hand, the clean one sees his companion is dirty, and thinks he is also dirty, so he washes."

"Oh, now I understand how Talmudic thinking works," says the man.

"Wait, I have another question," interrupts the rabbi. "Two men fall down a chimney. One comes out clean and the other comes out dirty. Which one washes?"

"This is the same question," protests the man.

"No, it's completely different," insists the rabbi.

"All right, the clean one washes," says the man.

The rabbi replies, "No, you missed the point. How is it possible for two men to fall down a chimney and only one comes out dirty?"

On your journey to discover Judaism you will have a myriad more questions than the 50 we address in this book. But it's a start. Why, you may ask, are there only 50 questions, and not 100, or 200, or even more? It's 50, because this number is significant in Jewish history. We read in the biblical story of the Exodus (chapters 15-20) about G-d's liberation of the Jews from 210 years of harsh slavery in Egypt. After the plagues struck Egypt, culminating in the death of the firstborn among humans and animals, Moses was able to lead the Jews through the Sea of Reeds into the desert to freedom. After seven weeks, they arrived at Mount Sinai, where G-d gave the Torah to the Jews through the hands of Moses, his Prophet. This became the Festival of *Shavuot*, the Festival of Weeks. Why did the Jews have to travel seven weeks (49 days, corresponding to the Forty-nine Gates of impurity of Egypt from which one can return, as opposed to the last one, the Fiftieth Gate) and endure all kinds of hardship right after their liberation from Egyptian slavery? Because right after this they still had the mentality of slaves. They needed time to become free not only in body, but in mind and spirit as well. They accepted the Torah at Mount Sinai as free people and gladly took it. Out of free will. True converts will need to travel through a "desert" like these early Jews and study, asking themselves if they want to break with their past to join a people who have known persecutions and trouble in history; a people set apart from all other nations. Also, a people which follows many complicated rules, has an extremely complicated lifestyle, and is so much in awe of G-d, that they do not even write His name in full but omit a letter, in order not to trespass against one of the Ten Commandments, "You shall not use the Name of the L-rd your G-d in vain!" Therefore, we spell the divine Name as G-d, or the L-rd, or simply as the Eternal or the Almighty. Or *HaShem*, which in Hebrew means The Name.

Through our queries we provide an overview of the content we consider an introduction to developing a meaningful Jewish life. These include core religious beliefs, observance, and culture. We cannot deal with these topics in-depth here, but there are a host of resources available to accomplish the goal of comprehensive learning. We just want to whet your appetite, and as we suggested above, we hope that you become enthused about learning regardless of whether or not you ultimately embrace Judaism. In the pages that follow, we include some traditional notions of Jewish life and religious practice. Our intent is not to persuade you to adopt an Orthodox or non-Orthodox perspective, since we do not believe there is only one correct way of practicing Judaism that must be carefully adhered to by all Jews. We stress that the Orthodox way, whether adhered to strictly or not so strictly, is the continuation of the Judaism we received from Moses on Mount Sinai, which has kept Jews together over several millennia. It is extremely important to know the Orthodox way so you can understand the foundation of Judaism. The Reform and Conservative ways may be less demanding in our modern society, but also an attenuation of traditional Judaism. We'd like you to know about the derivation of traditional practices. For example, if you understand the structure of an entire Shabbat Worship Service, were you to join a Reform congregation, you will be able to appreciate not only where various prayers come from, but you will also be able to recognize which have been abridged or were eliminated altogether. You will also see that despite many differences in practices, pronunciations, Hebrew reading or speaking, and clothing styles worn by Jews of various persuasions, there is a great deal of commonality as we stand beneath the big tent. Or, as we are fond of saying, we have a lot of colors in our box of crayons.

This book is intended for those with an interest in Judaism who are considering conversion to Judaism, or have already made the decision to become Jewish by choice but have not as yet completed the process. The perspective we offer is somewhat of a departure from previous works, and may appear debatable to some of our more traditionally minded co-religionists. But we look at the big picture of our society here and now, and that means that we deal with the fact that not everybody is Orthodox. Or wants to be Orthodox. The view we offer is informed by an appreciation for our history, knowledge base, and traditions. We formed our conclusions by asking the question: "How can we be authentically Jewish in a modern world?" Like many Jews, we've wrestled with this question for years, alternating between more Orthodox and more humanistic or secular leanings, trying to find our personal paths. On the pages that follow we anticipate the reader will ask the same question, presumably realize there is no one right way of being Jewish, and then discover her/his own path wherein Jewish practices and beliefs can provide a pathway to finding true joy in living.

Throughout the text we refer to ourselves by our first names. We believe this makes the book more of a conversation with real people, and that's important when dealing with such a personal topic as one's spirituality. When there are times each of us has a differing point of view we identify this in the text. We don't believe we have a monopoly on truth, and whether you see that we differ from one another, or that you arrive at a completely different opinion than the ones we've presented, you are free to question, and find alternative answers (but not alternative facts). Just so you know who we are and our individual perspectives, we'd like to give you a little background information on us.

Shoshannah was born in Holland to parents who survived the Holocaust. They were educated and assimilated into Dutch society, like many Jews before the Second World War. The harsh economic and social realities in Western Europe after the Second World War dictated that this was so. Consequently, they were not observant—that is how we characterize a Jew practicing his/her religion—, although they identified as Jews. In her youth, Shoshannah made the decision to become a *ba'alat teshuvah*, or someone who returned to her Jewish roots and embraced Orthodoxy. This produced something of a challenge, inasmuch as in her efforts to receive the best education possible where she lived culminated in her attending a Catholic school. Despite—or actually, thanks to—the challenges, she maintained her identity and currently identifies herself as Modern Orthodox, although she has deviated from the path in some of her practices. She pursued Jewish themes in both her writing and art. She got a PhD in Jewish Studies in Holland (Leyden University) which was uncommon, because the perspectives for employment in that field aren't great and the Jewish community of Holland is small. Therefore, she moved to Berlin, where she taught Jewish studies. After her marriage to a New Yorker, she became part of the large and diverse Jewish community of that city, and was ordained as a Maggidah, a traditional Jewish teacher and storyteller. She is an artist, author, and scholar. She returned to Berlin recently.

Bruce was born in Brooklyn, to parents who were the children of Orthodox Eastern-European immigrants who remained *Shomer Shabbos*, or traditionally observant, until adulthood. His father remained so until he joined the US Navy during the Second World War, where he was exposed to a great deal of diversity. His mother's family were Chassidim until they came to America, and gradually became more secular and assimilated. He grew up on Long Island, and his family became mostly culturally Jewish, and essentially non-practicing. Bruce recalls that as a child his grandmother came to visit for a week and brought her own pots, fearing her daughter's kitchen was insufficiently *kosher*. For most of his adult life, Bruce considered himself simply Jewish by birth, until he had a religious epiphany, returned to Jewish practice, and studied for the rabbinate. Today, he does not identify with any branch of Judaism, thinking this to be divisive, and is very liberal in his approach to Jewish thought and Jewish practice. The term post-denominational is often used to describe such individuals. Both of us had secular higher educations—Bruce took a PhD from Duke University,—which shaped our bias toward critical thinking, our belief in such concepts as evolution, and our relationship to the non-Jewish world. We both see ourselves as being blessed to live in a world filled with diversity of thought, culture, arts, race, and religion. We do not always agree on the answers to the questions in this book, but we both respect diversity. We study together and discuss our points of view the Jewish way. Jews usually don't agree with each other, but they do love dialogues. We are no exception.

Maggidah Shoshannah Brombacher, Berlin, Germany
Rabbi Bruce Forman, Plantation, Florida

Fifty Questions

1. What does it mean to be Jewish?
2. Who is a Jew?
3. What is the essence of Judaism?
4. What is Jewish spirituality?
5. How are women viewed in Judaism and how do they view themselves?
6. Why should I convert?
7. Is it easy to convert?
8. What is involved in conversion?
9. Do I have to take classes or can I just learn on my own?
10. What are my options for learning and can I learn online?
11. Are there any advantages/disadvantages to becoming Jewish?
12. Is there a difference between Chassidic, Chabad, Orthodox, Conservative, Reform, and Reconstructionist?
13. Why are there so many denominations?
14. Which denomination is the best?
15. Is it better to have an Orthodox conversion? Why is this so?
16. How long does conversion take?
17. Judaism has a lot of rules, like eating *kosher*; do I have to follow all of them?
18. Do I have to go to Synagogue Services?
19. Do I have to learn Hebrew?
20. What goes on during a Jewish Religious Service?
21. Do Jews read the Bible in Temple?
22. Why is there Antisemitism?
23. Will I be confronted with antisemitic stereotypes and strange beliefs?
24. Will people hate me if I become Jewish? How do I deal with Antisemitism after I convert?
25. If I convert but stop practicing am I no longer Jewish?
26. What is a *mikvah* and will I have to go in one?
27. I'm already circumcised. Will I need a *bris*?
28. Can I be part of the Jewish community if I don't convert?
29. Can I keep my Christmas tree when I convert?
30. Why do I need a Jewish name?

31. How will I be tested?
32. What if I change my mind about converting after I've started?
33. How much will a conversion cost?
34. Why was I turned away when I first inquired about conversion?
35. Will I be accepted in the Jewish World if I convert?
36. Will my children be Jewish?
37. What are Jewish lifecycle events?
38. Will I have a *Bar* or *Bat Mitzvah*?
39. Why do I have to do more than people who are Jewish by birth?
40. Are there saints in Judaism?
41. What does sitting shivah mean?
42. Do Jews believe in an afterlife?
43. If I have a tattoo, can I be buried in a Jewish cemetery?
44. What is the Jewish belief about forgiveness?
45. Do Jews believe the Bible (Torah) is literally true?
46. Why don't Jews believe in Jesus?
47. Why does the Sabbath fall on Saturday instead of Sunday?
48. Do I have to grow a beard? Must I cover my hair?
49. Does "Jew radar" really exist?
50. Once I finish conversion do I have to do anything else?

Concluding Comments on the future of Judaism.

About the Authors and some suggested readings

The Questions

1. What does it mean to be Jewish?

This seems like it should be a fairly straightforward and easy question to answer, right? You may have heard the old joke that says, give me two Jews and I'll show you three opinions. So, actually it is not that easy, because there are differing opinions. First, we can say that being Jewish means belonging to a religion, because Judaism is a religion. Alternatively, we can say being Jewish means belonging to a People and a culture. Which perspective is correct? Our answer is: they are both right.

As a religion, we can say Judaism was the first religion to espouse monotheism. There is evidence that an Egyptian pharaoh named Akhenaton, whose son was Tutankhamon (aka King Tut), believed in one (main) godhead, in this case, the sun-god Aton. However, Judaism was the first religion to fully embrace that belief. Jews rejected a pantheon of different gods for different fields and tasks in a world that took a pantheon simply for granted. The Jews worshipped an invisible G-d in a time and age where every godhead was depicted, as a statue, an image, or a natural phenomenon, like celestial bodies, holy stones, lightning, and rivers or trees, which were all worshipped. This set the Jews apart from everybody else in the Antique World and it did not always make them beloved. In certain respects, Jews wanted to be like everybody else in their known world. For instance, at one time they demanded to be ruled by a king, and not by judges, as had been the case until then. The story contained in 1 Samuel, chapters 11 and 12 describes Saul being anointed as the first king over Israel, but it states specifically: (1 Samuel 12:14): "If you fear the L-rd and serve and obey Him and do not rebel against His commands, and if both you and the king who reigns over you follow the L-rd your G-d—good!" The Israelite king had less power this way compared to the despots of surrounding countries, who could basically do whatever they wanted, and were in certain cases considered divine or having divine origins, like the Egyptian pharaohs. The Sumerian king Gilgamesh had so much power over his subjects and abused them in so many way just because he could, that even the gods were appalled and set up a scheme to reign in his ways.

There are more unique features of Judaism that set it apart from other religions. For instance, Judaism is a religion that—right from the start—espouses high regard for our fellow humans—even slaves, who in olden times were considered by non-Jews mere chattel—and respects animals and the environment. For instance, it is forbidden to chop down the fruit trees when you conquer the land and city of your enemies (Deuteronomy 20:19). In his seminal work *The Guide of the Perplexed*, Maimonides talks about ethical prescriptions expected of Jews being a way of improving relationships between people that acknowledges and respects the rights of others. This includes injunctions to be honest in one's business dealings. Additionally, there is the Law of *Lashon Hara*, literally meaning "evil tongue," which requires avoiding saying anything which could harm another person's reputation, even if true, such as engaging in gossip or spreading falsehoods. Violation of the Law of *Lashon Hara* is considered to result in the spiritual death of three people: the one who is being spoken ill about, the one doing the speaking, and the one who listens. To show how severely *lashon hara* is punished and how it invokes divine wrath, Moses' own sister Miriam, who had saved him from drowning in the River Nile, was struck with a skin disease (named *tzoraat* in the Torah) after slandering Moses' Ethiopian wife, who was Black (Numbers, chapter 12:1-10).

Importantly, Jews do not proselytize or attempt to convert others, as we do not believe we have a monopoly on truth. It is accepted that we, the Jews, have the Torah, but different people have a (large) share in different types of wisdom and serve G-d in their own way.

The Quran (*Surat al-Baqarah*) absurdly depicts Jews as monkeys (and in other *surahs* Christians as pigs) because they rejected the teaching of Mohammed in favor of clinging to their own beliefs, which irritated Mohammed a great deal. Having listened to Jewish teachers, his new concepts showed a lot of Jewish influences. But it wasn't Judaism, of course. And therefore, the Jews rejected his new religion. The Protestant reformer Martin Luther pronounced similar antisemitic views when he realized that the Jews were not interested in adopting his version of Christianity.

Some have said that Jews are a race. But that is a little extreme and does not fit the definition of race established by scientists. We share many common genetic traits with other Semitic Middle-Eastern people, like the Arabs. It was fairly common for Jewish communities in different parts of the world to mix to a certain extent with local populations, so they have some of these genetic traits as well. But to say that Jews are a people makes more sense. In the Torah itself, Jews are referred to as a *people* (the Hebrew word '*am*) or *nation*. Given our tribal origin, shared language, social rules, and shared heritage, certainly during biblical times, this is an accurate depiction. Although we acknowledge that there is no universally accepted definition of the term "*a people*." Jews usually identify both with their own ethnic/religious group and with the non-Jewish country of origin or where their ancestors sometimes lived for many generations. For instance, the Jews along the German River Rhine have been there for over a thousand years. Before the Second World War, those Jews called themselves Germans of the Mosaic Faith, but after the Holocaust, which proved that living in Germany for over a thousand years doesn't necessarily make you accepted as a German by all other Germans, many refer to themselves as German Jews, not Germans. And Jews from Poland or Russia are called—and call themselves— Russian and Polish Jews, not Jewish Russians or Jewish Poles, due to an exclusive position in a society marred by Antisemitism, whereas in the US one can say s/he is a Jewish American or simply American. It's very complicated to be a minority. History and the socio-economic position in a given country determines how Jews define themselves other than "Jewish." Whole bookcases were filled with works on this subject.

2. **Who is a Jew?**

A Jew is someone who has a Jewish soul. In traditional circles, this is passed on through a Jewish mother. This is similar to defining a *kosher* animal, which must be born to a *kosher* mother with certain characteristics, like split hoofs and chewing the cud, as found in cows, sheep and goats, or comes from an egg laid by a kosher bird, such as a duck or a chicken. Scientists are able to breed pigs with split hooves who also chew their cud, which is the biblical requirement for defining a *kosher* animal. But since they are not born to *kosher* mothers, we will never see a *kosher* pig, despite this variant having characteristics of *kosher* animals. Now we have the question what does it mean to have a Jewish soul? Does having a Jewish soul mean that one is more observant?

No, having a Jewish soul has nothing to do with observance, because the assimilated Jew (Jewish by birth) who never attends Synagogue Services, drives on Shabbat, or eats pork is just as Jewish as the Yeshivah student from a Talmud academy with a beard, black hat, and long black coat who studies all day. Similarly, having a Jewish soul has nothing to do with formal learning, because the Torah scholar is no more Jewish than someone Jewish by birth who has no Jewish education whatsoever. Having a Jewish soul may or may not manifest itself in any noticeable way, which makes this question so difficult to answer. For one who is Jewish by birth there is nothing that must be done; nothing that must be demonstrated. In fact, one does not even have to accept her/his Jewishness and even if rejected, Jewish law holds that the apostate remains a Jew. This is the religious view. The rabbinate in Israel considers only those people Jewish who have a Jewish mother and either adhere to the Jewish religion or no religion (see Questions #15 and 24), or underwent a strict Orthodox conversion, for the purpose of obtaining citizenship. But the Israeli government issued a court ruling in March, 2021 which now grants citizenship to those converted in Israel by non-Orthodox rabbis as well. This is different, however, from being able to marry or be buried in Israel, which is regulated by the Orthodox rabbinate. We will say more later about this extremely complicated situation. Until March 2021, Israel did not recognize conversion other than strictly Orthodox ones in order to avoid disputes. Orthodox conversions are recognized by all Jewish denominations, whereas non-Orthodox conversions are not.

There are times when it is apparent that someone has a sense they have a Jewish soul trapped inside a non-Jewish body. They feel compelled to convert to Judaism. So, if they already have a Jewish soul, why is it that they cannot just proclaim they are Jewish and leave it at that? The answer is that we have no way of verifying the presence of a Jewish soul, and they must go through some kind of process to prove that they do not only have a Jewish soul, but are also willing to live a full Jewish life. And what about born Jews who don't live a Jewish life? That's a different story. They do not have to prove anything. Outside of Orthodox and Conservative circles, in modern times the definition of having a Jewish mother has been extended to one who has either a father or a mother who is Jewish AND that they were raised as Jewish. If not, for that person to become Jewish requires going through some kind of acceptable conversion program that systematically explores Jewish practices and a body of knowledge.

The reason that the father does not count when determining who is a Jew has to do with the fact that before DNA paternity tests, one couldn't prove with a 100% certainty who was the biological father. But the identity of the mother is known because she gave birth. Women were sometimes raped or sold as slaves in olden times and gave birth to children of non-Jewish men. In addition, the mother is the one who usually influences the infant and young child most, and instills in her children a sense of who they are spiritually. It is generally believed that the mother passes on Jewish consciousness "with her mother-milk." We know the Torah story of baby Moses, who was put afloat in a basket on the River Nile to escape Pharaoh's murder squads coming for Jewish babies. However, Pharaoh's daughter herself found the basket, and she adopted the child. Moses' sister, Miriam had been keeping an eye on the baby in the basket from a distance, and when Pharaoh's daughter sought a wet nurse, Miriam stepped forward and suggested her own mother. Unbeknownst to Pharaoh's daughter, Miriam's mother was also Moses' mother, who then raised him with her *kosher* mother's milk until he was old enough to be brought to the palace of Pharaoh's daughter. Moses obviously had a Jewish soul, but he did not have a Jewish upbringing since he lived under Pharaoh's roof. But the seeds had been planted in his heart and mind. According to a *midrash*, a post-biblical explanatory religious story, Pharaoh's daughter later converted to Judaism and took the name Batya, meaning the Daughter of G-d. The daughter of Pharaoh is considered as Jewish as Moses himself after her conversion.

People who want to convert for sincere reasons have a Jewish soul already, longing for expression. But they must make it official for the world by studying, undergoing a qualifying examination, being tested by a *Beit Din* on sincerity, values, and knowledge similar to anyone seeking to become a member or citizen of any club, country, or organization. Have you ever tried to take a book out of a library without a library card that states who you are and which community you belong to? Or legally cross a border without documents? Since that is impossible, how could you expect to join a synagogue just saying that you are Jewish, without proof?

3. What is the essence of Judaism?

It is most important to recognize that there is only one G-d. This one G-d created and takes care of the whole universe. He made a special covenant with His children, the Jews, whom He liberated from Egypt and gave them the Torah at Mount Sinai. It is strictly forbidden to follow other gods or worship anything or anybody but the One true G-d. This is expressed in the quintessential prayer that is recited at least twice a day: *Shema Yisrael, HaShem elo-haynu HaShem echad*, Hear, oh Israel, the L-rd is our G-d, the L-rd is one (Deuteronomy 6:4). This essential prayer stresses G-d's oneness and the unique relationship between G-d and Israel. Most Jews, even if not observant, are familiar with this prayer.

Another essential point in Judaism is to love your fellow human. Once, Rabbi Hillel was approached by a heathen who wanted to learn Torah while standing on one foot. This sounds kind of strange and was actually an indirect way of asking for an abridged explanation. Rabbi Hillel said, "What is hateful to you do not do to others. All the rest is commentary." This gets at the essential aspect of Judaism saying that we should be loving to others, which is contained in the directive to love our neighbors as ourselves, contained in the Torah.

Rebbe Nachman of Breslov, the great-grandson of the Baal Shem Tov, the founder of the Chassidic movement, once said, "G-d loves when a Jew performs *mitzvot*. But he likes it a little better when those *mitzvot* involve other people." From this we learn not only the significance of following divine commandments, but also insight into an inherent hierarchy of those commandments. Following the laws is important, although it is not possible to follow all of them with perfection. It appears, at least to this Chassidic master, that those commandments that value human beings are more favored by G-d. If we follow the ideal that we should love our neighbors as much as we love ourselves this might be considered preferable in G-d's mind than praying with a *minyan* in a synagogue, for example. A fair society built on social justice is one of the essential points of the Torah, as stated in Isaiah 1:17: "Learn to do good. Seek justice. Help the oppressed. Defend the cause of orphans. Fight for the rights of widows." These groups usually included the poorest and most powerless people in ancient societies. The biblical prophet Amos admonished the people:

Forasmuch therefore as your treading is upon the poor, and you take from him burdens of wheat: you have built houses of hewn stone, but you shall not dwell in them; you have planted pleasant vineyards, but you shall not drink wine of them. For I know your manifold transgressions and your mighty sins: they afflict the just, they take a bribe, and they turn aside the poor in the gate from their right. (Amos 5:11,12)

And:

I hate, I despise your Festival days, and I will not smell [the fragrance of the sacrifices] in your solemn assemblies. Though you offer me burnt offerings and your meat offerings, I will not accept them: neither will I regard the peace offerings of your fat beasts. Take you away from Me the noise of your songs; for I will not hear the melody of your string instruments. But let judgment run down as waters, and righteousness as a mighty stream. (Amos 5: 21-24)

Both loving one's neighbor and observing the *mitzvot* involving rituals are important, but if we had to choose one or the other, maybe we should choose the one we think G-d would prefer us to do.

Another way of looking at Jewish practice is to consider how it may be derived. We wear a *kippa,* fix a *mezuzah* at our doorpost, and perform *mitzvot* so that we can maintain a sense of G-d's presence around us. For when we are mindful of the Divine Presence we have an awareness of G-d's love for his favorite creation, human beings. When we have this consciousness about others we will treat them as G-d treats us, with love and respect. And this is the best way of honoring our Creator.

While it is valuable to observe Jewish laws, follow rituals, and pray regularly, we believe all of these practices are aimed at just one thing. And that is being a good person, who is loving to others. That is emulating our Creator, Who is a good and loving Father for His children. If we pray fervently and follow the letter of Jewish law but fail to be caring and loving to other human beings, we fall short of living what Judaism has at its core. We illustrate this with a Chassidic anecdote about the Kotzker Rebbe. He did not have a high opinion of a certain colleague, whom he called "a *tzaddik* in a fur coat." While it is common in Eastern-Europe to wear fur coats in winter, he referred specifically to this stingy man, because he wore his thick coat inside the house to stay warm. But if he would have lit a fire in his room, everybody in the house would have benefitted, not only the man with the coat. The lesson is that you have to be considerate of others.

Loving your neighbor is important, but from a theological point of view there is more, of course. The influential medieval rabbi and scholar Moses Maimonides (aka Rambam) has formulated Thirteen Principles of Faith which contain the essence of Judaism. In Jewish thought, these are considered eternally valid and recited daily. They have also sparked a myriad discussions, explanations and commentaries by religious scholars. In short, they are:

1	G-d is perfect, the Primary Cause and Creator.
2	G-d is absolute and has no equal.
3	G-d has no corporeality.
4	G-d is eternal.
5	One must pray only to G-d and not worship idols or other gods.
6	G-d communicates through prophets.
7	Moses our Teacher is the greatest and most important of these prophets.
8	The origin of the Torah is divine.
9	The Torah cannot be changed or altered.
10	G-d is omniscient and provident.
11	There is a divine reward and punishment for humans.
12	Moshiach (the Messiah) will come to redeem humanity.
13	The dead will be resurrected in the messianic era.

4. What is Jewish spirituality?

Inasmuch as it differs across cultures, there is no generally accepted definition of spirituality. Consequently, we prefer a definition of spirituality as referring to one's connection with G-d, Divinity, a higher energy, or the sacred. It may also involve searching for insights or significance in life. Jewish spirituality comes from struggling with the mundane in ways that transform or link us with the divine Jewish spirituality is about *kedushah*, or holiness, which is interpreted as venerating the Divine and bringing G-d into the conversation or finding the presence of G-dliness, meaning and purpose. The Torah says, "Be holy because I, *Hashem*, am holy" (Leviticus 19:2). This implies that everything we do must be imbued with a sense of holiness.

In a Chassidic story, a pious man sweeping the floor feels he is engaged in a holy act. Is sweeping the floor a holy work, then? Not specifically, but you can make it holy by performing your (menial or other) tasks while concentrating on G-d and making the world a better place. You can sweep to benefit other people. There are many tales about Chassidic Rebbes performing lowly and mundane tasks in a way that compares them to the Temple priests in Jerusalem preparing a sacrifice for a Holiday. In his book *Jewish Spiritual Practices*, our teacher and mentor, Yitzhak Buxbaum, argues that almost anything can be a spiritual act if done with the proper attitude, or *kavanah* (intention).

Another example of how we approach spirituality in Judaism is to consider the *Motzei*, the prayer over bread. We take something mundane—grain—that comes from cultivating the earth. We manually process it, mix it with other ingredients, and turn it into bread. The act of saying a blessing recognizes the role of the Creator in the "magic" of growing the grain and giving us the wisdom and skill to change it into something that will nourish and sustain our bodies, so that we may perform divine commandments, which represents the essence of human purpose. The act of making this blessing transforms bread into something holy, because consuming it enables human beings to serve the Almighty and draw down holiness into the material world.

The purpose for which human beings were created was to make an abode for G-d in the physical universe. We often call our body a *mikdash me'at*, a little Temple, and we have the obligation to take good care of it. A *mikdash me'at*, according to the Talmud (Megillah 29a), is the holy space we create for the Almighty. And the only suitable place for G-d is a world that has been made holier through the participation of human beings. In Christianity, particularly in Catholicism, which has roots in Judaism, this ritual is contained in the

Eucharist, or Communion, that includes both bread and wine. Here, bread is transformed into holiness through the corporeal presence of divinity represented by the bread. But the distinction that makes a difference is one's consciousness during the act. Sure, we can go through the motions and say the blessing while preparing to eat the bread. Unless we approach the task with the intention, or *kavanah*, to fulfill an obligation or have awareness that we are trying to draw down holiness and bring it into our world, or sensing the presence of G-dliness with the aim of furthering our connection with our Creator, it is void of spirituality. The *rebbetzin* (rabbi's wife) of the Berditchever Rebbe was known to be an immensely spiritual and pious woman. Every Friday she baked two *challot* for each Shabbat meal. *Challot* is the plural for *challah*; it is customary to have two braided loaves set out for a Shabbat meal in commemoration of the double portions of manna provided to the Jewish people during the forty years spent wandering in the desert. People heard her say, "May *HaShem* give my husband the same holy thoughts when he makes *Kiddush* (the blessing over wine) and *Motzei* (the blessing over bread) as I have when I knead the dough for these *challot*." This wasn't bragging, something that was utterly foreign to her. She really felt that way. For her, kneading the dough was a sacred act. In this regard it makes sense that spiritual pursuits may take a variety of forms. They begin with having an awareness of the *Shechinah*, the Divine Presence. Expression of Jewish spirituality may be as simple as having the intention of performing a *mitzvah*, a divine command. Jews do not believe the road to Hell is paved with good intentions. Instead, we hold that if one truly intended to perform a *mitzvah*, but the task was not completed because of intervening circumstances, there is some merit due. It may be likened to getting partial credit on a math exam for having the right concept, but making an error in calculation preventing arriving at the correct answer.

Jewish spirituality may be articulated by the act of praying. Fervent, heartfelt prayer is preferable to praying by simply going through the motions. But even then, there is merit. And, despite some of the mind-numbing speed we've witnessed at some Orthodox *shul*s, it is never proper to *daven* (pray) rapidly. But what kind of prayer is valid, however, can be illustrated with this sweet Chassidic story.

A Chassid decided to visit his Rebbe. But it was a long trip from his house to his Rebbe's town and he had to spend a night at an inn. Fortunately, many guesthouses in Eastern-Europe were run by Jews, so Jewish travelers could always get *kosher* food and exchange the latest news. The Chassid arrived early and ate supper with the other travelers, who discussed matters of Torah and were happy that such a learned Chassid had joined them. They also talked about their towns, trades, and their families, as travelers love to do.

The next morning, the Chassid prayed his morning prayers together with the other guests, in a *minyan*. But something strange happened! The night before, the guests had spoken clearly and understandably. Now, the words of the prayers, which the Chassid knew very well, sounded garbled and unclear, like water rushing over pebbles in a brook. After they finished, the Chassid asked one of the travelers a question. He got a clear answer. Aha, he thought, they still could speak in a normal manner! He went to another guest and said quickly, in a soft, murmuring voice:

"Werurygoigtdy?"

"Excuse me, what did you ask?" answered the puzzled man. The Chassid repeated: "Wurarygongtd?"
The man stared at him.
"I am sorry, I still don't understand you!"
"Of course you don't," retorted the Chassid, "I said, *Where are you going today* just as fast and as garbled as you mumbled your prayers. Is this how you talk to the King of Kings, to G-d, the Ruler of the World?"

The man understood what the Chassid meant. He hung his head and apologized. All the travelers stood in a circle around the Chassid and promised from then on to pray differently, to pay attention, have the right intention, and pronounce the words clearly, even if they didn't always understand all the Hebrew words, because they were merchants, not scholars. They thanked the Chassid for his simple but profound lesson, ate breakfast together, and went their way.

The Chassid visited his Rebbe. On his way home his heart was light, because soon he would see his dear wife and his little boy whom he had missed so much.

His wife opened the door with their toddler son on her arm. He stretched out his pudgy little arms and gurgled: "Gooaaghhgoogoo." "Ah, my little *bubbaleh* (sweetheart)," answered his mother, "I will get you some porridge, come!" and took him to the kitchen. The Chassid was amazed. "How do you know he wants porridge? Those *goohgahs* and *gagagoohs* sound all the same to me!" "But not to me," said the mother with a smile, "I am with him day and night, so I know exactly what they mean. I learnt this lesson when I was praying in Hebrew, which I find very difficult: G-d knows what we want, because we are His children, even if our speech or knowledge of Hebrew is not perfect, as long as we are

sincere. Don't worry, our baby will grow up, we will teach him the right words, and soon he will talk as clearly as you and me! It is our task to teach him!"

Attending Services at a synagogue or *shtiebl* (little private place of worship) and participating in a *minyan* (quorum of ten Jews) is generally desirable, but some prefer to *daven* alone where they can meditate. That way they feel they are communing more closely with the Almighty. For instance, the Chassidic Rabbi Uri of Strelisk preferred to *daven*, pray, alone, by himself, because he found the people in his *shul* lacking *kavanah* (intention), knowledge, and

decorum. When he found a strong admonishment in the Talmud that one must *daven* with a community, he handpicked nine men and invited them to his house, so he could pray with a *minyan*. Still not satisfied—because he felt that the way other people *davened* might be good for them but it interfered with his own particular way—he resumed *davening* alone again. Then he heard a *bat kol*, a "divine Voice," telling him he *must daven* with a community. Now he could no longer refuse and exclaimed: "I will do that, and if *HaShem* had ordered me to pray with wooden book lecterns, I would have done that as well." How you *daven* depends more on your intention than on your environment, even if the latter disturbs your concentration.

A community provides spiritual support, irrespective of the spiritual level of those assembled or distracting habits such as talking, fidgeting, or humming while others are *davening*. Orthodox rabbis actually demand that somebody who wants to convert live in and with a Jewish community for some time, preferably for life. In other words, Judaism is not something you know, it's something you live.

Meditation, even if it is separate from prayer, is also a Jewish way to sense the connection with G-d and heighten the experience. Chassidic masters often set aside time to meditate and be alone with G-d in order to commune with Him, termed *hitbodedut*. Some, like Rabbi Nachman of Breslov, made long walks in nature for this purpose. The Baal Shem Tov withdrew into the mountains. Others emphasize Torah study as their path to expression of spirituality. Study for its own sake is merit worthy. However, study with the purpose of having Torah teachings more fully integrated into one's consciousness and behavioral repertoire in everyday life is more desirable. Study leading to assuming additional *mitzvot*, or to *tikkun middot*, developing character traits, such as enhanced ethical principles, action to right social wrongs, or simple charitable acts or giving are even more meritorious. One's presence, thus assisting with the burial of someone who died is a spiritual act too. Presence at a wedding celebrating with the bride and groom are *mitzvot* as well. Attending a funeral and throwing dirt over the casket during the burial is considered a *mitzvah chesed shel emet,* an act of true selfless kindness, inasmuch as one can never be repaid for this kindness. So, it is done purely for the benefit of the soul of the deceased. This, too, belongs to the realm of Jewish spirituality.

For most people, the goal in life is not to become saintly. Rather, it is to identify the saintliness that already exists inside each one of us and to bring holiness into the mundane aspects of our lives. We all have holy sparks within us. Our challenge is to find ways of translating them into action and living meaningful lives. At the same time, we also have a kind of brokenness; a fractured relationship with the Almighty. Surely this is true, if not exacerbated, if one smokes cigarettes or eats or drinks alcohol too much, or pursues other (self-destructive or vain) activities earmarked by self-gratification. But we can be healed. Broken spirituality is a natural and normal process that occurs inadvertently and automatically for most human beings. Spiritual healing must be implemented intentionally. We are obligated to transform mundane acts into something sacred and change negativity into something positive. An interesting example is found in the ancient belief that people are born under the influence of the planet that is prominent in the sky at the hour of their birth. This planet supposedly influences a person's character. For instance, the planet Mars was named by the Romans after the war-god Mars and considered to produce belligerent children. The Jews called the red planet Mars *ma'adim*, the "reddish one" and associated Mars with shedding of blood. Does this mean that those born "under Mars" are doomed to be at best warriors and at worst murderers? No, such a person can channel an inherent barbarity into something useful, and even holy, for the community and become a *shochet*, (a *kosher* butcher) or a surgeon. Holiness can be attained by repurposing belligerence into providing chickens for Shabbat tables or healing the sick.

5. How are women viewed in Judaism and how do they view themselves?

To answer this question, you need to look at different times in history as well as different communities. In the Torah, Jewish women have rights. The five daughters of Zelophehad, a man who died without male heirs, asked Moses questions about the laws of inheritance (Numbers 27). Would their father's inheritance "disappear," or would it go to his own daughters? Moses decided in their favor on condition that they marry men from their own Tribe and the property stays within the Tribe. This decision was critically important, since it underscores the comparability of sons and daughters in the orderly transmission of property from one generation to the next. Compared to their sisters in other cultures, Jewish women were protected by Torah law. Of course, times were different and movements like Women's Emancipation and Feminism had yet to be established. In the introduction, we mentioned the rights of female slaves and captives. Our modern eyes do not tolerate slavery and see things differently because our society has evolved. But Jewish women were and still are protected by ancient laws, for instance financially in the case of a divorce. Women are entitled to receive a minimum payment to provide for their support, as stipulated in their marriage contract, or ketubah. Biblical laws protect women from arbitrary divorce and maltreatment. Widows are protected. So, was everything ideal back then? No. Even today there are ancient laws in effect that grant a husband the right to divorce his wife for any reason, but the wife must come up with specific reasons. Laws chain an abandoned wife to a meaningless marriage in case the husband (in-)voluntarily disappeared and can't be traced to give her a bill of divorce, called a *get*, or dies without witnesses confirming his death, thus preventing her from remarrying. And in many societies being doomed to live in poverty. Whereas a husband in a similar situation may remarry, albeit not without a complicated procedure. The Torah protects and values women. She is often praised as the stronghold of the family, making a house a home and raising her children to be honorable people (*menschen* in Yiddish). The *"Woman of Valor"* (Proverbs 31) is sung every Friday evening and describes a skilled and praiseworthy woman in a society where everything and everybody has a specific role, women do strictly women's things and men have their own territory. And in some circles, like the Ultra-Orthodox, this is still the case.

Additionally, women are considered more spiritual than men. In a *midrash*, a comment on the Torah, Jewish women refused to give up their jewelry to make the sinful golden calf in the desert, but the men did. Later on, the women gladly offered their most prized possessions, copper mirrors, to fashion the wash basin for the priests at the Tabernacle in honor of the One True G-d. In the mystical Sefirot tree, a collection of ten Attributes of G-d, men are connected with *Chokhmah*, wisdom, but women with *Binah*, insight. Women possess an innate intuition that men are lacking. Women are supposed to raise their children as G-d-fearing Jews and not give in to idolatry, but if they do, their sin is considered worse than when men do the same, because women have more spiritual power. An old saying states that a good woman can make a bad man good, but a good man cannot make a bad woman good. In many cultures, men adore women but they are secretly a bit afraid of them and therefore assert and exaggerate their influence outside of the house, making a dominant impression. In Judaism, all this has been regulated by laws, but men are only human.

In older patriarchal cultures, attitudes on how to treat women—and how they view themselves—greatly differ from our modern and emancipated ideals of equality and equal chances. Jews not only follow Torah Law, but are influenced by the mores of their countries of residence and their time. For instance, the great medieval Torah scholar Maimonides lived in Egypt. He stipulated that women should not be too educated and stay home, not being allowed to go out more than one or two times a month to visit relatives or attend a wedding. He was influenced by the strict Sharia laws and customs of the Muslim society in which he lived. Another great medieval Torah scholar, Rashi, lived in France. His daughters were educated Torah scholars themselves and women in his community had their own businesses. Torah Law is binding but interpreted in as many different ways as there are societies. In some communities, like the early Chassidic *shtetls* (Eastern European towns with a considerable Jewish population), women were exempt and often barred from serious Torah study because they had to take care of young children and household chores, before the invention of convenient washing machines and the like. This was in addition to supporting the family with a small business, because their husbands strove to be full-time learners, which meant earning no or little income. Since learning Torah was considered the highest pursuit for Jews, women were treated with less respect than men. There is a moving story about a Chassid who loves his devoted, pious and hardworking wife. One day, he learns in his *beit midrash* (study hall) that a pious wife will be her husband's footstool in the next world. He goes home and cries. If my dear wife can't sit next to me on a chair, he challenges the Eternal, then I don't want Your hereafter. I won't allow my dear wife to be a footstool.

In our time, we have different challenges. The first woman to get *semichah* (ordination) and be inaugurated as a rabbi was Regina Jonas in 1935 in Berlin, of course not in the Orthodox community which still rejects female rabbis on historical and halakhic grounds. There is a breech in this concept. In several modern Orthodox communities, women called "rabba," despite lacking ordination, fulfill a function similar to rabbis. In non-Orthodox circles female rabbis are common.

All of this is connected to broad possibilities for women in modern Western societies to access a higher education. Shoshannah has a PhD in Hebrew studies. Her grandmothers did not finish High-school, but were supposed to help at home and in the family business, marry, and raise a family. One of them was happy with that, the other one wasn't but made sure her daughters would have opportunities not available to her. In Chassidic circles, many women still work in jobs that do not require extensive study or training, and are also devoted to raising a family. This is a huge and demanding job due to the large number of children many of them have.

Now, there are famous female politicians, like Golda Meir, scholars like Aviva Gottlieb-Zornberg and Nechamah Leibowitz, and female professionals in fields that were formerly reserved for men. Historically, there always have been female politicians and scholars, but not in large numbers. To mention a few, the Bible describes the judge Devorah, the Talmud the erudite Beruriah, and in Chassidic circles there was a scholar who taught Torah to men, the Maiden of Ludomir, which says something about her knowledge in these circles.

The perception of women by men who interpret the laws, such as rabbis, depends largely on how these men perceive and deal with women on a personal and social level. If they have a happy marriage and live in a country that views women favorably and values them, then they are inclined to make different decisions, compared to when their relationship with women is bitter. What's new? The famous kabbalist Isaac Luria (aka the Arizal) worded it this way: *The person to whom our Torah speaks is neither a man nor a woman, but both combined. For this is how Adam was first created and this is how we are in essence: Two half-bodies that are truly one. The minds are two, but the bodies, the souls and the very core of these two people are one and the same. This is why the character and responsibilities of a man and a woman differ, for each side of the body does its part to compliment the other. It would be redundant, after all, for both sides to do the same.*

And how do Jewish women nowadays perceive their own role in Judaism? It depends, like everything else. There are Orthodox women who are perfectly happy with sitting separated from men in the synagogue and not being called up to read from the Torah, because they know the historical reasons for these laws and customs, and feel respected, not put aside. In Shoshannah's modern Orthodox shul in Brooklyn, men and women socialize during *kiddush* after Services and women can give a *dvar Torah*, a lecture about a religious subject, just like men, but not during Services. Other women feel more at home in a non-Orthodox synagogue where they basically do the same things as their male counterparts,

including wearing a prayer-shawl (*tallit,* traditionally worn by men), and reading from the Torah in public, like in the shul Shoshannah attends in Berlin. Women's roles within Jewish families are highly individualistic as there is not one correct way to be a family. There are still glass ceilings for women in the corporate world, and also in the Jewish community. But a lot depends on one's beliefs and perspective.

Some rituals are exclusively for women, like in Orthodox circles mandatory visits to the *mikvah (*ritual bath) after menstruation and counting seven "clean" days. When a person knows the reasons behind these laws and customs it becomes clear that they have nothing to do with an "inferior position" or being "unclean," but actually give the woman power to regulate her own sexuality. At an Orthodox wedding, the *chatan* (groom) offers a *ketubah* (signed marriage contract) to his *kallah* (bride). By accepting that and a ring, she accepts him as her husband. She doesn't have to do anything else. Orthodox men wear no wedding band, their wives do. In non-Orthodox circles, two rings are exchanged and both groom and bride sign the contract. People do what they feel comfortable with. We discuss this in our book about wedding customs, *Under the Chuppah: A Jewish Coupe's Guide to Weddings and Meaningful Marriage.*

The bottom line is that men and women are different. Obviously, we don't have to explain that. Therefore, they are subject to different laws and customs in Judaism. But both are respected and commanded to respect each other. They are partners. An old *midrash* explains why Eve was created from one of Adam's ribs (Genesis 2:22) and not from his head, because she might feel haughty, or from his feet, because she might feel lowly. She was created from his rib, so she would be close to his heart. In Genesis 21:12, Abraham was commanded, "Whatever Sarah tells you, listen to her voice." According to the Zohar, an important kabbalistic text, a king without a queen is neither great nor a king. The Lubavitcher Rebbe commented that the woman empowers the man to conquer his space. And it is the man who empowers the woman to penetrate and nurture hers. And then the man will learn from this woman that he, too, can reach within others and provide nurture. And the woman will learn that she, too, can conquer.

6. Why should I convert?

This is a very personal decision. But we want to share a humorous story with a serious undertone. You have to know that until as recently as the twentieth century there was a broadly held taboo against marrying a non-Jewish partner, thereby "betraying" the "group." The Jewish minority wasn't always accepted or looked upon with friendly eyes by society at large. Even Jews who were not observant preferred to look for a spouse in their own trusted community, for social reasons. Jews are like many other people who prefer a partner with a similar background. And if somebody did choose a partner outside of the Jewish community, it was often expected that this partner would convert to Judaism, so that the children could be raised in a Jewish home.

Josh, a young Jewish man whose family was not observant, comes home with his girlfriend to make an announcement. He introduces Kelly to the family, and says that although she is not Jewish they are planning to get married. "It'll be fine, she's converting." Grampa, with a scowl on his face, whispers in Josh's ear, "Don't marry the *shiksa* [demeaning term for a non-Jewish woman], you'll be sorry."

Josh and Kelly proceed with their plans. Kelly goes through an Orthodox conversion followed by a big wedding, standing under the traditional Jewish wedding canopy, the *chuppah*. Kelly takes her Judaism seriously. One day, Josh pays a visit to his family. He tells them, "She's driving me crazy. We have a *kosher* home, observe all of the holidays, including ones I've never heard of, and on Saturdays I have to walk to Services and I'm not allowed to watch TV."

With a smirk on his face Grampa says, "See, I told you not to marry the *shiksa*."

Conversion as we know it now is not biblical in its origins. There are biblical stories of conversion, like the *erev rav* (literally, the rabble-rousing ruffians we call riffraff, same word) who accompanied the Hebrews leaving Egypt during the Exodus. Some say their descendants converted during the period of Mordechai and Esther (who are associated with the story of Purim in ancient Persia). And there is the biblical Moabite woman Ruth, of course, who is the model of sincere converts. Scholars tell us that the first evidence of formal conversions began roughly 2200 years ago during the Hasmonean period in Israel, when Greeks ruled and Hellenism was spreading. Today, conversion is sought for a number of reasons. One of the most common reasons for converting is that someone has met, fallen in love with, and wants to marry a Jew. This is a fairly common situation in the US in modern times. In fact, the intermarriage rate is over 50%. Another reason is that someone has decided on her/his own, that Judaism resonates with them, and is the right spiritual path to follow. For many rabbis, the second one is the preferred reason to become Jewish, and for Orthodox Judaism the only valid one, although those who convert for a spouse are often accepted if they show a sincere interest. This may sound a bit odd, but for Shoshannah and Bruce, converting to Judaism for marriage is actually something we think should be encouraged for the long term good of the Jewish people to remain a distinct group. Beginning in ancient biblical times, when the Jewish people consisted of Middle-Eastern tribes, there was a tradition that marriage outside of their own Jewish tribe was discouraged. Jewish tribes were relatively friendly and cooperative with one another, but differences remained. If there was a marriage between two people from different tribes, inheritance—especially land located within one's own tribal territory—became very complicated, and kinship ties and loyalties could become fragmented. As Jewish tribes coalesced, kinship bonds extended to all other Jews; a kind of "us" and "them" mentality. With the exception of the priestly Tribe of Levi, which produced the Kohanim (priests) and the Levites who served in the Temple, Jews are unable to trace back to which tribe they belong any longer. Whoever is no Kohen or Levi is "just regular Jews." But now, there are still (big) cultural and social differences between Jewish cultural and geographic groups, and not every Ashkenazy (Western or Eastern European) Jew will easily marry a Sephardic (Mediterranean) or Mizrachi (Middle-Eastern) Jew. Initially, conversion to Judaism was easy and not discouraged, as in the case of Ruth, for instance. Ultimately, as the religion became more sophisticated and complex, there was a legitimate concern that newcomers would not be knowledgeable or worse, would stay loyal to their own idolatrous rites and customs as well, especially in the case of (inter-)marriage, and entice those Jewish from birth to follow their heathen practices. We find strong warnings about this in the Torah, for instance in Deuteronomy 13:7-11. This way, the religion would be watered down, or spouses and children would be led astray to serve foreign gods. The same concerns apply to Reform conversions in other than Reform circles, and therefore Reform conversions are neither accepted in Israel for the sake of citizenship, nor in Orthodox communities for the sake of being recognized as Jewish. Another problem was the fear that converts might want to return to their origins. Whatever reason they may have, they might turn against the Jews, which as a minority were vulnerable. These renegade converts would have too much inside knowledge and endanger the Jewish community. This has happened more than once in history, unfortunately. So, rabbinic leaders put up barriers to becoming Jewish. Through the centuries, the Jewish people became insular and did not mix with other groups, which also often had conditions to join them and demanded to give up one's Jewish religion. Eating only *kosher* food from *kosher* vessels doesn't help either to fraternize with people who do not eat *kosher* food nor do they use *kosher* pots and pans, like non-Jews. Over time, being a community only marrying their own, there was a great deal of inbreeding—especially in isolated geographical locations—resulting in a number of conditions that are tied to genes and genetic mutations. Our position is that if we invite others to join our religion and marry Jews, the gene pool benefits by the addition of variety. We see this in Israel, where members of hitherto geographically separated communities meet and marry, like Yemenite Jews with Ashkenazim from Russia, although there are also many people who prefer marrying a partner with roughly the same cultural background. And that's fine. As a result of enriched and expanded genes the Jewish people are ultimately ensured of healthy survival.

7. Is it easy to convert?

Usually conversion involves four elements:

- some degree of formal learning,
- demonstration of a commitment, as shown by making changes in lifestyle to include Jewish observances,
- review of status by a clergy in a religious court referred to as a *Beit Din*, and
- a ritual to finalize the process.

How closely the conventions are followed depends on who is responsible for managing the process of conversion. In Orthodox circles, this is a rabbi who assembles a panel of other clergy called a *Beit Din* (literally: house of judgment), usually consisting of three rabbis. But not just any rabbi will do, just like with specialized lawyers, it is often a rabbi who specializes in conversions, as there are rabbis who specialize in divorce and overseeing laws of *kashrut*, assuring compliance with laws governing food and its preparation. Within other movements of Judaism, the conversion process may be handled by a rabbi or a cantor. Some synagogues have formal programs to assist those wishing to convert. There are also independent rabbis who supervise the conversion process, and tailor the requirements to individual needs. For example, someone who has been in an interfaith marriage for several years, living in a home where Judaism has been practiced, and then makes the decision to formally convert because s/he is planning a family, may need a less rigorous program of learning than someone who is new to Jewish culture.

Someone seeking an Orthodox conversion may be required to spend upwards of two years to complete the conversion process. Ideally, learning continues for the rest of one's life. In Orthodoxy, one is required to observe all the *mitzvot*, the 613 precepts of the Torah, many of which are complicated and require a lot of study. In mainstream circles, which in the US means Conservative, Reform or Reconstructionist, it is more likely to be six months to a year. Several years ago, there was one rabbi in Miami Beach who offered a one-day conversion class. It may sound funny, but Bruce has known some of the graduates of this express immersion program, and they seemed to embrace Judaism as much as those who came out of lengthier programs. Their knowledge of Judaism may not have been that extensive, but in their hearts, they were committed Jews. And they caught up on studying subsequently. Like many others who are serious about Judaism and hold it near and dear to their hearts, we have trouble taking this highly abbreviated process seriously. We believe that one can only truly be committed to Judaism when one knows what he or she is getting into, by studying and learning the ideas, laws, and traditions contained in our vast collection of written works. This rabbi's son received ordination and continues the work his father began. While he has detractors among the mainstream rabbinate, he is beloved by many in the South Florida community he serves. This is reminiscent of a Talmudic story about the famous Rabbi Hillel (who lived during the first century before the Common Era or BCE), known for his practical and very gentle approach to people who asked him questions, Jews and non-Jews alike. Once, a gentile came to ask the rabbi to explain the Torah to him while he, the gentile, was standing on one foot. Instead of sending him away and rebuking him for such a ridiculous request, Hillel answered: "What is hateful to you, do not do to your neighbor. That is the whole Torah; the rest is the explanation of this—go and study it!" The operative words are contained in the last part of this sentence. Of course, if you want to become Jewish you have to go and study before you can make an educated decision to join the Tribe. And that takes a lot more time than you can stand on one foot.

8.   **What is involved in conversion?**

As noted above, there are four basic components of conversion. First is the formal learning. This involves most of all learning Torah, Jewish history—including learning about Antisemitism—and laws, biblical Hebrew, prayers, customs, ethics, and Shabbat and Holiday observances. The degree to which one is exposed to all of the content will vary according to where and with whom conversion study takes places. A rule of thumb to follow is that the more traditional and religious the path, the greater the time spent on in-depth learning. A value that runs through all branches of Judaism is that embracing Judaism involves a love of learning, and a desire to learn more throughout one's life for personal growth and enhancement. So even—or better said, especially once conversion is completed—there is an implicit expectation, often expressed explicitly by the rabbis during the *Beit Din*, that it is just the beginning of a life-long process to not only acquire knowledge, but to apply each new bit of learning to life in an effort to improve our character and become more spiritually elevated. This is in fact expected from every Jew, born Jewish or a convert. You might appreciate that even though Shoshannah and Bruce, who are both Jewish by birth, have been studying Judaism for many years, we continue to learn and evolve. Our perspective is that if we live for 120 years, and study faithfully every day, we will still not know all there is to know about Judaism. This is illustrated by a Chassidic anecdote. Men strive to study the whole Talmud during their lifetime, which is a major

project that many may never complete. But it's the effort that counts. Even if it's "completed," there is always so much more to study.

Rabbi Levi Yitzchak of Berditchev explained why each volume of the Gemara traditionally starts with *daf* (leaf, folio) 2. There simply is no *daf* 1. This way nobody can boast, or even claim, that he studied a large amount of *Gemara*, because he hasn't even completed the "first page."

We take our lead from the teachings of Rabbi Tarfon, a Talmud scholar who in the *Pirke Avot* (*Ethics of the Fathers*) taught, "The day is short, the work is never ending, and the taskmaster is harsh." This has been interpreted to mean that just because we can never perfectly follow all of the commandments, and can never master all Jewish teachings, we are not exempt from doing the best we can to accomplish as much as we are able to. There is another Chassidic story that illustrates this point.

Rabbi Zusya, a famous but humble Chassidic master, was on his deathbed, crying. One of his students asked him why he was crying, surely, he was not afraid of death? Rabbi Zusya replied: "When I get to Heaven, the Almighty will not ask me why I was not as hospitable as Abraham, because I am not Abraham. And He will not ask me why I was not humble like Moses, because I am not Moses. He won't ask me why I wasn't learned like the Rambam (Maimonides), because I am not the Rambam. He will ask me why was I not like Zusya. Why was I not the best I could be? And I don't have an answer for Him."

It is not sufficient to simply learn the teachings of Judaism. Rather we must integrate them into our daily lives, and be the best human being we are capable of being. In the Talmud, someone whose learning is great but does not act on the knowledge is likened to a tree with shallow roots. It wouldn't take much to topple that tree. Similarly, it wouldn't take much to get a learned but non-practicing person to give up on Judaism. During the conversion process, daily practice of Judaism must be integrated with learning. Depending on the level of observance, daily practice may begin with learning the prayer said upon awakening, i.e., *modeh ani*: "I gracefully thank you, O living and Eternal King, for You have returned my soul within me with compassion—abundant is your faithfulness," and all the morning prayers said at home and during Worship Service, or may include an abbreviated version. Learning must include those prayers said at home, as well as those used during daily Prayer Service. On Shabbat, Holidays, and Festivals there are many other observances in addition to prayers. These differ from daily practices. Not only converts go through this process but also *ba'aley teshuvah*, those born Jewish who did not grow up with all the details of Judaic practice but become religious later in life, so they had to learn them afterwards, or those who did grow up in a Jewish atmosphere, but left the path only to return later in life. One of the reasons why it takes longer to complete the Orthodox conversion process is because it is considered necessary to go through at least one annual cycle under supervision. Which is a good idea if you want to get a more authentic experience.

Because the convert (or *ba'al teshuvah*) usually has many questions it is imperative that s/he studies with a competent teacher and has a Jewish friend, or study partner, with whom to discuss what s/he has learned. Two millennia ago, that book full of wisdom called *Ethics of our Fathers* urged us to do just that. Even great rabbis must have a *chavrusa* (study partner) and a rabbi they can consult.

Once the conversion candidate completes directed learning and begins to integrate Jewish practices into daily life, a recommendation will be made by her/his teacher to appear before a board of rabbis, or other clergy, to determine readiness for completion. Except in Orthodox circles, it's something of a formality and is also a time for the conversion candidate to reflect on her/his spirituality. Bruce has served on a conversion *Beit Din* several times, and though he usually asks the candidate to reflect on her/his personal meaning of being Jewish, he found that questions had to be tailored to each candidate's situation and level of understanding. What is most important is the candidate's sincerity and *kavanah*, or intention. In one instance, a candidate was not really ready and had to be admonished to go back to learn more, and return when he was truly ready. That got his attention, and he took his study more seriously.

The conversion process is completed by engaging in a conversion ritual. This is known as the Ceremony of *Tevilah* [immersion]. The cornerstone of this ceremony is immersion in a *mikvah*, a ritual bath, and saying a specific blessing. This means that the candidate gets completely covered in water that comes from a natural source and is free flowing. There must not be any buffer or obstruction between the person and the water. First, one takes a shower to be sparkling clean, clips one's nails and combs (untangles) one's hair. Not only clothes, but also jewelry (like earrings) and makeup, band-aids, even possible dirt under one's finger-nails, must be completely removed. In most communities there is at least one *mikvah*, which is constructed according to a set of complex rules. Until recently—and in some case still—Jews use(d) rivers, lakes, or the sea as a *mikvah* if no man-made and clean, heated ritual bath is available in their small communities, even in the dead of winter. There are moving stories about secret *mikvaot* (plural of *mikvah*) in communist Soviet Russia and the great trouble people took to fulfill this precious—but then forbidden—*mitzvah*. In Bruce's home in South Florida the ocean is often used as a *mikvah*. Bruce once served on a conversion *Beit Din* and brought the candidate out on his boat in Biscayne Bay, along with the candidate's wife and the rest of the *Beit Din*. After the immersion they docked at a local bar and celebrated.

9.   Do I have to have to take classes or can I just learn on my own?

Learning is valued wherever and in whatever manner learning it takes place. Being on a quest for lifelong learning about Judaism and the refinement of one's character has long been considered an important goal among Jews. Our belief is that what kept the Jewish people going for so many centuries, against all odds of survival, was the Torah. Learning is the key to our perseverance. In order to know and understand what is needed to keep religion and culture alive we must study Torah. "Torah" in this context is all of the sacred texts, not just the Five Books of Moses contained in a Torah scroll. In addition, Torah study involves the Oral Law, known as Mishnah, as well as commentaries on them, which is known as Gemara. Together, Mishnah and Gemara comprise the Talmud, a large work in many volumes, containing 63 tractates. In addition, there is study of Jewish laws, called Halakhah, plus commentaries on them. Then there is the study of prayers and rituals within synagogue services, along with learning the Hebrew language. Self-study through the internet or by any means is certainly encouraged, as is learning with a *chavrusa*, or study partner, as is done traditionally in learning Talmud. However, learning under the guidance of a teacher is preferred, because someone who is not knowledgeable may miss the important elements needed to complete conversion. Teachers have long been revered among Jews, because they played a vital part in not only the transmission of learning from one generation to the next, but because this learning was considered essential to our communal wellbeing and survival. This is one reason for the time-honored tradition of so many Jews becoming teachers. In some areas of American culture, those who aspire to become teachers are considered less intelligent people who end up in low paying and unrewarding jobs. But Jews have historically held teachers in high regard, and respect those who pursue this career for the contribution they make to society. Several people in Shoshannah's family followed this path. Although he has a law degree, Shoshannah's husband proudly chose a career enabling him to shape young minds as a public school teacher in New York City. Shoshannah's grandfather in Holland was a teacher. Her father was the head of a laboratory and a researcher, but assumed a teaching role as a professor at a university because he loved teaching students. Shoshannah herself lectured at the Free University of Berlin and still gives lectures. Bruce had an academic career when he was a young adult and while he aspired to be a researcher and scholar ultimately found his most significant role was as a teacher. He now takes great pleasure in working with those studying for conversion.

Because the conversion process requires someone to serve as a mentor and shepherds the candidate through the conversion process, it is not possible to complete conversion totally on one's own. In fact, Judaism emphasizes life in a community, preferably with a

family that is part of that community, and a personal rabbi/teacher. Most rituals, prayers, and in general Jewish life takes place within a group of people. Learning is no exception. For centuries, Jews have been studying in groups, with a study partner, and in classes. Even the greatest rabbis, who are teachers themselves, take pride in having a teacher. Some people might prefer to study part of the time by themselves, but no Jew studies completely alone. Bruce and Shoshannah were study partners in their course to become a maggid(ah), a Jewish spiritual teacher and traditional story teller. And they continue studying together until this day.

10.　What are my options for learning and can I learn online?

As technology evolves, it has become increasingly acceptable to learn in non-traditional ways. A generation ago it was considered inappropriate, even scandalous, to get a college degree without attending classes on a campus. Accusations of diploma mills were made. Today it is different. Universities that once looked down their noses at non-residential approaches to learning are now profiting from the trend and even leading the way with new course offerings. During the COVID-19 pandemic we got used to courses, lectures, and the like on Zoom and it is unlikely that this way of teaching will disappear after the pandemic abates. Bruce, who lives in Florida, and Shoshannah, who recently moved form New York to Berlin, have been studying virtually together for years. They know each other in person, of course. Today, it is possible to earn a legitimate accredited undergraduate, master's or even a doctoral degree without setting foot on a campus. So, too, Jewish learning has changed. Today, it is possible for one to learn Judaism through online classes, since we are the most wired generation that ever existed. But you will still need the guidance of a live teacher who will recommend actual experiences and readings. Many synagogues offer conversion programs that involve attending classes. They usually require students to attend services for Shabbat and High Holy Days and religious study along with other activities like readings, attending Jewish theater, films, exhibits, or museums. Interactions and discussions with others going through the conversion process are also considered beneficial. You can read about that in Rebbetzin Pessie Stein's enlightening novel about a group of converts and how they interact and solve questions and problems, entitled *Jews for Joy*.

As we've emphasized, being part of a community is essential. There are online Jewish communities, groups, and organizations, but that is not enough. Judaism doesn't believe in hermits or solitary recluses. Most rituals, including prayer, are performed best with some or even many people. Some prayers and reading from a Torah scroll can only be said or done with a *minyan*, a quorum of ten people (reading the Torah from a book is always possible, of course, even when one is alone). Marc Zborowski wrote a book about the culture of the nineteenth century Eastern-European *shtetls*, Eastern-European towns with a large Jewish population and a distinct Yiddish culture. The book is titled *Life is with people*. That's what Judaism is about. This became even more evident during the Covid-19 pandemic. The seder meal for the Pesach holiday is one of the highlights of the Jewish year and celebrated with as many guests, friends and relatives as you can seat around your table plus a few more. On Pesach, no Jew eats alone, by him or herself. But many people who were quarantined during Pesach 2020 and had no choice but to eat their seder meal alone or with just one or two people living on their home, found ways to connect via social media, like Zoom.

Shoshannah's rabbi in Brooklyn said that this was the first time in his entire life that he celebrated a seder with just two people, he and his *rebbetzin* (a rabbi's wife). Shoshannah and her husband had no guests either, nor did Bruce have guests.

11.   Are there any advantages/disadvantages to becoming Jewish?

There have been periods of time when Jews experienced considerably greater Antisemitism in the world than exists in America today, although—as we all know too well—it has never been away here, too, and is currently reemerging very rapidly. Yet, Jews continued to bemoan the fact that they were Jewish because they continued receiving mistreatment at the hands of non-Jews, who were the majority in virtually every community where Jews resided in the Diaspora, or *Galut* (outside of the Land of Israel). Interestingly, until the second World War Jews were relatively well treated in the Muslim world, with notable exceptions even in the Iberian Golden Age. Jews understood their Judaism to be who they were as human beings and not just a religion they could choose to practice. In other words, being Jewish was part of the fabric of who they were ethnically , culturally, emotionally, morally and religiously, even culinary. This explains why the Jews were considered "a different people" in countries like Poland and Russia. In the Soviet Union with its plethora of ethnic groups, like White-Russians, Tatars, Uzbeks, Kazakhs, etc., one had his ethnicity stamped in his passport. For a Jewish person, it stated "Jew." Today, many of us still feel the same way, we identify as Jews first and as Americans, French, Dutch, etc., second. This might be a difficult concept for converts who embrace the spiritual side of Judaism but are still steeped in their secular family origins, which are not Jewish. In the USA, one is often asked, "Where were your ancestors from?" A Jew will answer that they were Jews in Poland, Russia, or any other country, whereas a non-Jew might simply answer that they came from Poland, Russia, Ireland or Italy.

Once, a Jewish man was invited by a Black neighbor to accept Christ as his savior and become a Christian. The Jew told this well-meaning neighbor that he could no more become a "real" Christian than the Black man could stop being Black. The German poet Heinrich Heine (1797-1856) lived in a society which barred Jews from many positions and careers as well as from full participation in society. So, he did what quite a few other German Jews had done and would continue doing until World War II: he got formally baptized. Not because he preferred the Christian religion over his ancestral Jewish beliefs, but because, for him it was "the ticket of admission into European culture." However, a Jew remains a Jew, baptized or not. At the end of his life he wrote the famous lines, "They won't say *kaddish* [the Jewish prayer for the dead] and they won't sing a Mass [for me]." He felt that he belonged neither here nor there and wasn't fully accepted by either group, Jews or Christians. Although according the Jewish theology it is possible to do *teshuvah* (to come back and repent) and be accepted by G-d, in the eyes of people it's often a different story. Once a Jew, always a Jew, whether that is favorable or not. Once a renegade, always a renegade in the eye of some.

According to Jewish tradition and Jewish law, if a Jew renounces Judaism and stops practicing in favor of another religion or no religion, s/he is simply regarded as an apostate, but is still regarded as Jewish, belonging to the Jewish people at large. Famous examples are Karl Marx and Baruch (aka Benedictus de) Spinoza, or the Jewish nun Edith Stein. The latter was killed by the Nazis because she was ethnically Jewish (born to a Jewish family), even though she had formally converted to Christianity and lived with the nuns of her order in a monastery. The Catholic Church considers her a martyr. She is pictured in church windows, like in the Virginia G. Piper Chapel in Phoenix Arizona, complete with a yellow Jewish star sewn on her habit, as well as several German and other European churches. So yes, becoming Jewish definitely has some disadvantages.

Here's another anecdote. A Jewish man was persuaded to convert to Christianity by his well-meaning neighbors. The conversion process consisted of the local priest saying some blessings and sprinkling him with holy baptismal water. He was then pronounced Christian by the priest. One Friday evening, the man was seen at a restaurant by his Christian friends. To their horror he was eating roasted chicken. This is not permitted by the Church, and Catholics traditionally eat fish or eggs on that day to commemorate that Jesus died on a Friday and therefore, one should not have a festive meal with meat, in contrast to Jews, who do eat festive meals on Friday evenings to celebrate the onset of Shabbat. Even many non-religious Jews wish to preserve the memory of their grandmother's chicken-soup with *mandel* (croutons) by having a festive meal on Friday evening.

The friends of the newly converted Christian admonished him, and warned him that eating meat on Friday is a sin. The man looked at the delicious roasted chicken on his plate and replied, "Everything is fine. I told the chicken: "Chicken, you were meat, but now you are a fish," and sprinkled some water over the plate." They answered, "Dear man, have a good look, is that a chicken or a fish?" to which the renegade answered, "And I, am I really a Christian now or still a Jew?" Jews intrinsically belong to an ethnic and cultural group which you cannot change even if you change your religion. This might pose a problem for some converts, who are considered completely Jewish in the religious sense but not in the ethnic sense, although they are usually not told so to their face.

The Torah teaches that Jews are to be a holy nation of priests, who are enjoined to light the light of Torah, and especially to share the teachings about G-d to all other nations. Consequently, the Jewish people occupy a special position for G-d. Some Chassidic rabbis use the term *lamp lighters*, because we are a "light for the nations." Jewish people are referred to as "the apple of His eye," a term from Zechariah 2:8 and several other verses in Tenakh, like Psalm 17:8; Proverbs 7:2. So, you might conclude that being Jewish gives one a special position in the universe. And in some ways, it does. But there is a big price to pay. Early in the Torah we discover there are the Seven Noahide Laws. These preceded the giving of the Torah at Mount Sinai and the Ten Commandments. These seven laws govern, for example, how to treat G-d and one another, humane treatment of animals, and establishing a system of justice. To gain favor in G-d's eyes it was necessary only for a person to follow the Seven Noahide Laws. But then later on, we learn that this is sufficient for all the nations of the world, but not for the Jewish people, since they have accepted the great gift from G-d, the

Torah, upon themselves. Jews must follow the remainder of the commandments. So, for non-Jews there are only seven laws, but for Jews there are 613 laws with all their ramifications.

There are growing numbers of racial and ethnic groups who have embraced Judaism. Through advances in genetic testing and electronic access to genealogical records, we've seen those who did not live as Jews for centuries but suspected they had Jewish ancestry, like people with Sephardic Iberian/Spanish/Portuguese origins in Spain, Italy, Latin America, and South Florida. They are discovering their Jewish and "Marano" roots. Maranos were Jews forcibly baptized by the Spanish in 1492. This name given by their tormentors is demeaning and is connected to "pig." They prefer to be called *Anusim*, the "forced ones." Since the authenticity of their connection to Judaism, specifically their matrilineal descent which destinies if somebody is Jewish or not, may be in question after many ages and likely intermarriage, they have sought formal conversion to Judaism as a means of activating their connection to the Jewish people. Additionally, we have seen a burgeoning interest in Judaism among Black people. Many identify with the Hebrew Israelites movement. Many People of Color believe they have ancestral connections to Ethiopian Jews, who are said to be descendants of King Solomon and the Queen of Sheba. Their current chief rabbi is Capers Funnye, a cousin of former First Lady Michelle Obama. To ensure acceptance by the larger Jewish community, Rabbi Funnye went through a Conservative conversion (which means that his Jewish authenticity is still in question within Orthodox circles). While many Black converts participate  in these traditionally Black congregations, many also seek conversions and participate in existing Jewish communities. Unfortunately, Jewish People of Color face a variety of challenges due to a combination of Antisemitism and rampant racism in the US. In an anecdote from the sixties, a Black Jewish convert is reading a Yiddish newspaper in the subway in Brooklyn. The Chassidic man standing next to him gently taps his shoulder, and asks him, "Sir, if I may ask, being Black wasn't difficult enough for you?"

We don't believe the reactions of small-minded people should be a deterrent to finding one's spiritual path in life, although we do recognize there are times when it is an uphill battle, and we applaud those who have the courage to press onward. They are not the first ones. Moses' own wife Tziporah was Black and experienced racism from Miriam, Moses' own sister (Numbers 12:1). Miriam was severely punished for her prejudice, which is leading to the insight that racism has no place whatsoever in Judaism.

12. Is there a difference between Chassidic, Chabad, Orthodox, Conservative, Sephardic, Reform, and Reconstructionist?

To some non-Jews, Jews and their synagogues are different from everyone and everything else, but otherwise indistinguishable from one another. In fact, originally there was only one kind of Jew and there weren't any denominations. There were branches, like the Jerusalem and the Babylonian schools which had different interpretations and ways of doing things, but they all belonged to the one and only denomination that existed, namely Orthodoxy. Although, at that time this term was not in use, of course. Ultimately, things became complicated and enormous differences of opinion developed. This is one reason why studying Jewish history is important to developing a Jewish identity. In Biblical times, the Jewish people followed the written laws in the Torah fairly closely. Then differing perspectives developed, so that a council of seventy learned men, called the Sanhedrin, was formed to rule on matters of law. This Oral Law—equally given to Moses on Mount Sinai—was eventually written down between ca. 200 and 500 CE. In Hebrew this is referred to as *Torah she b'al peh,* literally Torah that is on the mouth, the orally transmitted Torah. Restatement of these teachings combined with discussions and debate about them, *Mishnah* and *Gemara,* is known as the Talmud. Owing to a variety of factors—like the destruction of the second Temple in Jerusalem in the year 70 CE and the end of the rulings of the priestly class—Judaism evolved into what we refer to today as Rabbinic Judaism, where the designated leaders (rabbis) interpret the laws and make decisions. Those who maintain this perspective wish to keep Judaism pure, so they hold on to beliefs and interpretations that have been in use for millennia but still keep developing, e.g., connected to modern technology, and are ruled on and interpreted with the help of the rules and methods found in the Talmud. They see to it that traditions are upheld and not watered down by the forces of modern society. These are known as Orthodox. For Orthodox Jews, the Written Torah (the Fives Books of Moses, the Pentateuch) and the Oral Torah (the Talmud) and their commentaries are equally binding. Of course, they make full use of modern society as well, but within the confines of what interpretations and guidelines are derived from rabbinic Law. This can be compared to the *midrashic* story about *Moshiach's* (i.e., the Messiah's) donkey. It carried several biblical figures on its back throughout history and finally will carry *Moshiach*, the one who will bring the Ultimate Redemption of the world. And who is this "donkey"? None other than the Torah, which kept the Jews together and supported them throughout their long history of exile and dispersion, bad luck and persecution.

There are groups among the Orthodox who take their interpretations and practices to the extreme with even more stringent views about what constitutes proper observance. These are the Ultra-Orthodox, or fundamentalists. Chassidim are a sub-group of the Ultra-Orthodox —who are for the greater part non-Chassidic but whose physical appearance may be similar, except that the Chassidim wear black hats and large fur hats called *shtraymels* and non-chassidic Ultra-Orthodox men wear black hats only, no fur. What sets Chassidim apart is that they were established in eighteenth century Eastern-Europe by the sage and *tzaddik* named

Israel ben Eliezer, aka the *Baal Shem Tov* (the Master of the good Name) and have integrated mysticism and a system of local leadership (rebbes) and unrestricted mutual aid with their different subgroups into their practices. Chassidim often point to exuberance and joy in living in addition to fervent worship. Ironically, the Chassidic movement started as a rebellion against the very strict intellectual religious establishment in eighteenth century Eastern-Europe. Back then, Chassidism was more lenient with certain rules and commands, making it attractive to simple, uneducated Jews. But nowadays, they are among the most stringent in their observance. Chabad is a Chassidic group that follows the Baal Shem Tov, whose ultimate successor after several generations of Chabad Rebbes was the Lubavitcher Rebbe, Rabbi Menachem Schneerson. He passed away in 1993 without having a son or appointing an other successor, like one of his students. His followers work tirelessly to bring back Jews into the Orthodox fold, especially those who did not or could not receive instruction in their religion, or those who left the path and want to return. They set up schools and "Chabad houses" to help any Jew in need, spiritually or otherwise, and extend help to non-Jews as well, for instance during (natural) disasters. Unlike most other Chassidic groups, they do not keep to themselves but reach out to all Jews. As Rabbi Schneerson liked to say, "We are G-d's salesmen."

During the eighteenth and nineteenth century two other main groups formed to redefine Judaism in their times. The Conservative Movement started in Germany in the nineteenth century. It is closely related to the civil emancipation of those German Jews who wanted to integrate their lifestyle and their style of worship with that of their non-Jewish German neighbors. They established practices and beliefs that were more contemporary and more German than traditionalists, though they conserved many of the older practices, such as following most laws of *kashrut* (eating ritually permitted food, like meat slaughtered in a certain way and abstaining from pork, shellfish, or other forbidden animals), while maintaining much of the theology. They prayed partly in German, partly in Hebrew, and shortened the lengthy Orthodox services in the synagogue. Their rabbis and cantors assumed the dressing style of Protestant vicars.

The Reform movement similarly began in nineteenth century in Germany. After an initial radical swing to the left wherein traditional practices were discarded altogether or replaced by German Christian practices, like introducing an organ and a choir in their synagogue—now called Temple—they moved to a more centrist position and revised both liturgy and theology on a scale never seen before. They did not insist on the purely divine origins of the Torah that was handed down to Moses on Mount Sinai, but speak about divinely inspired writings, which is something different. Their ideas sparked large controversies with Orthodox rabbis, who consider Reform Jews heretics until this day because they are breaking with the tradition that began with Moses on Mount Sinai. In Europe, Reform is referred to as Progressive and Conservative as Liberal Judaism. The Reconstructionist movement began in the twentieth century in New York, led by Conservative rabbi Mordechai Kaplan, who advocated for each generation to redefine Jewish practices and beliefs according to what is happening in the greater society.

Two other movements that developed during the twentieth century are Jewish Renewal, which emphasizes spirituality, and the Neo-Chassidic movement, which appeal to young, secular educated Jews who were not born in a Chassidic community. It must be noted that all of these branches of Judaism occurred within the Ashkenazy communities, in Western Europe and especially in Germany, and/or America. Mizrachi and Sephardic Jews are more closely aligned with the Middle East and, until Medieval times, with Spain. In fact, *Sefarad* means Spain, and Sephardim are descendants of Jews from the Iberian Peninsula. Middle-Eastern Jews are called *Mizrachim*. Sephardic Jews follow the same Torah teachings as Ashkenazim or Western and Eastern European Jews, but use a different liturgy, *nusach,* or rite. When chanting from the Torah, they use a distinctly different trope that produces melodies reminiscent of Islamic chants, where the Ashkenazim chants are heavily influenced by Western music. For instance, the melody of the famous Chanukah hymn *Maoz Tzur* ("Rock of Ages") was borrowed from a Bach Cantata. There are other distinctly Sephardic practices as well. It's often noticed that the Jewish head covering called *yarmulke*, or *kippah*, is worn by Sephardim mostly during Prayer Services, but Ashkenazim wear them all day, especially among, but not limited to, the Orthodox. Also, foods like rice and beans are permitted during Passover for Sephardim, but were strictly forbidden to Orthodox Ashkenazim and Conservative Ashkenazim until 2017. Sephardic Jews have no branches— such as Conservative or Reform— like the Ashkenazy communities. Their adherence to traditional practice is considered to be more closely aligned with Orthodox customs, or *minhagim*. There are many factors to consider when deciding which denomination is right for you, such as where you live, or plan to live, as well as the degree and kind of observance that resonates with you. There are also a number of smaller and splinter groups, some dating back to ancient times. Since they make up a very small percentage of Jews—and have what some consider aberrant practices, like, for instance, the Karaites, who follow only the Torah and reject interpretations that go beyond scriptural writings—it is very unlikely you will encounter them. But if you have an interest, feel free to learn more about these various forms of Jewish beliefs and practice and integrate what appeals to you. After all, it's your spiritual journey and you should find practices that are meaningful for you. Following observances because they are easy is not a good reason to embrace them.

13. Why are there so many denominations?

Jewish people, much like everyone else, have a variety of opinions. And they're not afraid to express them. While there are times when we find people who hold extreme points of view to be both annoying and amusing, overall, we find the notion that there is not one size that fits all to be comforting. G-d created us in His image, which is known as *tzelem Elohim* in Hebrew. As such, we human beings reflect the complexity of G-d and the many facets of His nature. So, we celebrate the variety of G-dly attributes expressed in humans as attesting to G-d's infinite variety manifest in the beauty of human ideas and styles. There is a concept called *The Seventy Faces of the Torah*, meaning that the Torah can be interpreted in various ways, even in a way that might seem disagreeable to others. Because we have a variety of approaches to the practice of Judaism we are almost assured that each of us will find the path that is right for us. And the good news is if we discover it doesn't fit as well as we imagined, we can change course. Orthodoxy is the oldest and original brand, based on following the Written and Oral Torah, both of divine origin, but since the nineteenth century there are many more variations. The concept of multiple approaches and interpretations is illustrated in a Chassidic story:

The Radoshitzer Rebbe once asked the Seer of Lublin about the right path to serve *HaShem,* G-d.

Answered the Seer, "There is no such thing as *the* right path to serve *HaShem*; there is a path of learning; there is a path of fasting; there is a path of eating; there is a path of meditating; there is a path of dancing; there is a path of studying; there is a path of singing, and there are many, many other paths! No two people are the same. We each have our own appropriate path. But the path that *YOU* choose you must follow with all your might."

14.   Which denomination is the best?

Since we concluded that there is not one path that is right for everyone, finding the best one is relative. What is right for Shoshannah might not be right for Bruce. What is right for us may not be right for you. Despite our differences in theology and observance, we do agree that no one branch of Judaism has the monopoly on the right or best understanding of what G-d wants, although Orthodoxy has the best claim to tradition and authenticity, and—for Shoshannah—is the authentic Judaism. Although she agrees that other branches made valid changes in certain practices. In fact, we not only acknowledge our differences, we celebrate them. Yet, some Jewish leaders insist that theirs is the one true path and that all others are misguided, if not just plain wrong. The late Lubavitcher Rebbe, Rabbi Menachem Schneerson from the Chabad movement once said, "There are those who mistakenly categorize Jews as religious and non-religious, but there are only religious and not yet religious Jews." Orthodoxy does not validate other brands, such as Conservative, Reform, or Reconstructionist, for understandable reasons. If one believes that the Torah in its Written and Oral form (the Talmud) is G-d-given and divine and all 613 *mitzvot*, or commandments, must be followed meticulously, it speaks for itself that those who change or ignore some—or many— of these commandments are not considered what Orthodox means, "on the right path," a Greek word composed of *doxa* (opinion) and *orthos* (right). Now, within Orthodoxy there are different interpretations of how to explain and follow certain rules and commandments, but that they must be followed is generally accepted. In our modern society, certain groups within Orthodoxy put the door ajar for female rabbis, but they don't call these women rabbis, although they perform many of the same tasks as male rabbis. In Conservative and Reform synagogues there have been female rabbis and cantors for quite a while, just like there are now female professors, engineers, or judges. Not everybody who identifies as Orthodox follows all the laws meticulously, people are human, but all agree they represent the ideal. One of the biggest commandments is to love one's fellowman like oneself, and not to humiliate him or her. Bruce was once horrified to hear an Ultra-Orthodox rabbi advise a congregant not to attend the wedding of a relative because she was Reform and Reform Judaism is not really Judaism. This is based on the fear of Orthodoxy that Reform is so watered down that it neglects key principles which have kept Judaism strong and alive for millennia. And that by following Reform Judaism, it might last only a few more generations. But Reform Judaism is more in sync with the changes of our modern society, our evolved philosophies and ways of thinking since biblical times. Another time a rabbi announced that it was forbidden to set foot into a Christian church because Christianity is idolatry, but this is beyond the scope of the different branches of Judaism, since Judaism and

Christianity are two completely different religions.

Like many people, we cringe when presented with opinions or having the wrong interpretation masquerading as facts. The Torah has 613 *mitzvot* (divine commands), but how exactly we interpret and observe them often leaves room for interpretations, and unfortunately, also for wrong interpretations or misunderstandings. The best advice we can give is to experience as much variation as you are able. Remember, too, the tone of what you experience in a synagogue comes from the rabbi. Two Chabad houses, while using the same books, will have markedly different energies, because each reflects the personality of the rabbi. The same is true for Conservative, Reform, Reconstructionist, or for that matter, any other kind of congregation. The Lubavitcher Rebbe once remarked that there are no "good" Jews or "bad" Jews (depending on their denomination seen from the point of view of another denomination), there are only observant Jews and not yet observant Jews. But read the next question carefully.

15. Is it better to have an Orthodox conversion? Why is this so?

Yes, actually there are advantages to obtaining an Orthodox conversion, but you may not agree with the reasons why this is so. There is an inherent hierarchy within the branches of Judaism that essentially follows degrees of observance. The more observant, the higher the status. At least in the mind of many Jews, especially those who think they are at the top of the ladder. Orthodoxy has a valid point to consider itself the legitimate heritage of Judaism as it began at Mount Sinai in the desert, several millennia ago. Through the ages there have been many changes in interpretation and adaptations making it easier to apply and obey Torah laws, but the core has been preserved: the Torah is G-d's own word which He gave to Moses on Mount Sinai to deliver to the Jews, who, by living according to the Torah, are partners in the Covenant between *HaShem* (G-d) and the Jews. Reform Judaism considers the Torah written by human beings, divinely inspired but subject to change if time, society, politics and customs demand so, therefore it cannot and will not be considered an equal or legitimate partner by Orthodoxy. This is an impasse. Orthodoxy will not capitulate to those who do not consider the Torah G-d's own word, independent of whether a Jew keeps all the laws meticulously or not. These Torah laws are explained by Orthodoxy as G-d's own words

written down—and copied exactly over the ages later on—by human hands with their own style and possible transcription errors, but the Torah is still considered G-d's own word that cannot be altered by any human being. The same applies to biblical prophecy; G-d puts His words in the mouth of the prophet, who then tells it to people in human language they can understand. Different groups among the (Ultra-)Orthodox might explain aspects of the Torah in different ways, but it is ultimately G-d's binding word. If the Torah tells you not to light a fire on Shabbat, which is "making a change from one substance or situation to another," this implies that you cannot use electricity to switch on the light on Shabbat, because then you also cause a change in a situation or substance (from no light to light or changing electrical energy into light). You can use modern techniques, like a time-switch, so that the light goes on and off "by itself" at the time you set the timer before Shabbat, but you cannot flick that light switch yourself after sundown on Friday evening. Is that utterly not practical in our time and age? Absolutely! And that's why Reform Jews permit you to put on the light switch, but by doing this they defy the underlying principle. Of course, one has to know all the reason(s) why you can't put on or off the light, it is a very complicated matter that we cannot get into here, but the bottom line is, for the Orthodox, ignoring or changing the laws is heresy at best and may lead to creation of a totally different religion at worst. In most countries outside of Israel, Orthodox and non-Orthodox Jews live side by side, and although they might not frequent each other's houses of worship they are all considered Jews. This is not the same situation in Israel. The fact is, that when the State of Israel was being formed—in 1948, shortly after the Second World War in which the Nazis had murdered six million Jews, wiping out whole families and communities—concessions were made with the (Ultra-)Orthodox rabbis, who wanted to rebuild the Jewish people from the ruins of Europe, for political expediency. Initially, anybody who claimed to be Jewish and did not adhere to another, non-Jewish religion was accepted but later, the Orthodox rabbis could define who is a Jew—and therefore has a right to citizenship—and they did so according to Orthodox standards. A Reform Jew born to a Jewish mother is therefore a Jew, but a convert who underwent a Reform conversion—which is not recognized by the Orthodox— is not. The situation in Israel has gotten out of hand so that now the Orthodox rabbis wield so much influence that other branches of Judaism have been relegated to second class status. For example, a couple cannot marry in Israel without the sanction of the Orthodox leadership, even if both partners consider themselves atheists but are technically Jewish by having a Jewish mother. Within the past few years, it has become more and more difficult to make *aliyah*, going to live in Israel, for converts who did not have a strict Orthodox conversion by a religious court, or *Beit Din*—Israeli or otherwise—that is approved by the Israeli rabbinate. Recently, the Israeli Supreme Court ruled that those converted in Israel by a non-Orthodox Beit Din are allowed to state "Jewish" as their ethnicity on their ID card (as opposed to, e.g.,

Arab, or non-Jewish) if they live already or plan to live in Israel, but that won't help them when they want to get married or be buried in Israel, because then the Orthodox rabbis who won't consider them Jewish have the power to deny them. A crazy situation, that will only become crazier when all parties involved start fighting each other, politically and religiously. In the US it's not as extreme, but the Orthodox still exert an undue influence that is disproportionate to their number, although it must be said that with intermarriage and assimilation being at an unprecedented high, the fastest growing group is that of Orthodox Jews. They make sure that their children get a Jewish upbringing and press them to marry a Jewish spouse and raise Jewish (grand-)children. The latest Pew survey found the Orthodox comprise about 10% of all Jews in the US, which is a relatively small number considering the entire Jewish population in the US is estimated at just over five million, or roughly 40% of the world's Jewish population. Another 40% reside in Israel, while the rest are dispersed throughout the world.

Despite their modest numbers, Orthodoxy remains the standard against which other forms of Judaism are evaluated. Many mainstream Jews look at how Orthodox Jews practice and judge themselves. We've heard Jewish people say things like "I'm not a good Jew because I don't keep *kosher*" or "I'm not as worthy because I don't go to synagogue every week." As we said already, Rabbi Menachem Schneerson, the late Lubavitcher Rebbe, once quipped, "There's only one kind of Jew. There are mere differences in degree of observance." From this observation we learn there is no real difference between Jews beyond how we practice. Still, when it comes to conversion, there is a hierarchy that cannot easily be broached. If one undergoes an Orthodox conversion there is no question in anyone's mind about how thorough the immersion into Judaism was. Someone who completes an Orthodox conversion will be accepted by rabbis in all other branches of Judaism. If the conversion was completed under the auspices of the Conservative movement, it will be accepted by the rabbis who identify as part of the Conservative movement and all others, with the exception of the Orthodox. If one plans on relocating to Israel, or wants to get married in Israel, only an Orthodox conversion will be acceptable. The mother, and therefore the female convert, determines the Jewish status of her children, which are only considered Jewish in Israel if she underwent an Orthodox conversion. Children of a mother with a Conservative or Reform conversion outside of Israel are not considered Jewish in Israel and cannot become citizens or marry a Jewish spouse in Israel. But even the credentials of the rabbis serving on the Orthodox *Beit Din* granting the conversion may be called into question. If you have serious concerns about how you will be perceived and accepted if you go through a non-Orthodox conversion you should speak with your rabbi or Jewish studies guide to assist you in deciding upon the right kind of conversion for you. All we can say is that most of the people we know who are not part of an Orthodox community develop a high degree of comfort with their non-Orthodox conversion, as they have a sense that their Judaism adequately serves their needs. Then there's another thing to consider, and that is how a convert is judged by his or her fellow Jews. Some people, notably those who are Orthodox and those who are less educated or biased (of any denomination), call people with an Orthodox conversion "real Jews" but not those with any other kind of conversion, although they have different reasons for doing so.

16. How long does conversion take?

The answer is, "It all depends." There are some generally accepted minimal standards and requirements in Jewish law that set out what a potential convert should learn or how long it should take. The decision about the length of a conversion program is highly individual, based on what the rabbi, cantor, or Judaic teacher thinks is appropriate. There are conversion programs that are as short as one day (although, as we pointed out earlier, it is hardly possible to take these seriously, unless it is a formal conversion of somebody who is already well versed in Judaism, like somebody who all of a sudden finds out that s/he is not halakhically (according to Jewish Torah law) Jewish, but was raised Jewish), and others that take a couple of years. If we had to guess how long it is likely to take you, we would say you should assume it would take at least a year or two to acquire the knowledge and go through all of the holy days with a new perspective. But learning does not stop after the *Beit Din*, learning is for life! And how serious the obligation of learning for life must be taken is illustrated by a story we mentioned before. It is useful to repeat it, because it is an important deep truth. The sixty-four treatises in the Talmud are numbered as *dapim*, (sheets or folios). The front of a *daf* (sheet) is number 2a and the reverse 2b, etc. But none of them is numbered *daf* 1a and 1b, a treatise always starts with *daf* 2a. The Berditchever Rebbe once said: "This way no one can boast that he has learned all of Gemara (Talmud), because he did not even study *daf* 1! Go and learn!"

We mentioned the well-known Reform rabbi in Miami Beach and his one-day conversion program. His son, who is a popular and charismatic rabbi, has followed in his father's footsteps and continues to offer one-day programs. While popular, such conversions are looked at with suspicion by the mainstream Jewish community and generally not taken seriously. Some synagogues have formal conversion programs that involve classes, lectures, and homework that take the better part of a year. The Darshan Yeshiva is an online program that allows students to watch a series of online videos and are then mentored by a rabbi (Bruce serves as one of their mentors). Students can finish this non-Orthodox conversion in a year or less, depending on their level of previous learning and participation in Jewish life. In Orthodox circles, the required time to convert is not specified but is usually completed within a two-year period. In most of Europe or other places with small communities it takes much longer, because often prospective converts lack a large community to assure greater learning and being absorbed easily. We believe the choice of where and how to complete the conversion process is highly personal and should be a well-considered decision. For instance, if you are in a serious relationship with someone whose family is Orthodox, then it is recommended that you pursue learning that will fit in with family values. A fundamental

tenet of Judaism is that it is a religion of **home and family** more than it is a religion of the synagogue, so this value must be taken into consideration when deciding on the way that is ultimately best for you. Conversely, if you are, or have, married into a family that is very assimilated and liberal in their practice of Judaism, it is not recommended to go much further in your studies or you risk alienating the family. In other words, you should ask yourself "What is in my long-term best interest?" or "What will lead to *Shalom Bayit* (peace in the home)?" rather than what is easiest or most convenient. But ultimately, we hope that you convert for love of the Torah and desire to become part of the Jewish people, of course.

17.　Judaism has a lot of rules, like eating *kosher*; do I have to follow all of them?

We do, indeed, have a lot of rules. We actually have 613 of them in the Torah, plus their often lengthy explanations and ramifications by rabbinical authorities. These are found in Jewish law codices. The word *mitzvah* means commandment. Then there are another seven additional ones that are rabbinic, meaning we have them by decree. They are the result of considered thought and there is agreement they should be followed. For instance, the post-biblical festival of Chanukah is not contained in biblical writings—the Jewish biblical canon doesn't include the so-called Apocrypha books, like Maccabees,—but it has become ingrained in Jewish culture, ritual and observances. In other words, we say it carries the weight of a Torah law. A contemporary rabbi, teacher, storyteller and singer, Shlomo Carlebach, of blessed memory, taught that we should consider the *mitzvot* as 613 beautiful and meaningful ways of connecting with G-d.

As we have noted before, in the *Pirke Avot*, translated as *Ethics of the Fathers* and a part of the Talmud, one of our sages, Rabbi Tarfon, said: "The day is short, the work is without end, and we have a harsh Taskmaster." Our understanding of this lesson is the recognition that it is not possible to flawlessly perform all of the *mitzvot* contained in Judaism. Some of them, like sacrifices, we can't possibly perform anymore because they were connected to the Temple service in Jerusalem, and that (Second) Temple was destroyed in 70 CE. There had been several decades without a Temple in Jerusalem earlier in history after the First Temple had been destroyed by the Babylonians in 587 BCE, and it took time to rebuild it. But the Third Temple will not be rebuilt until *Moshiach* (the Messiah) will come and redeem the Jews. And that hasn't happened yet. Other *mitzvot* are complicated for many people. But that doesn't absolve us of the need to do the best we can in trying to perform them. For Orthodox Jews, there are three very important sets of *mitzvot*: the laws of *kashrut*, which regulate what food is permitted to Jews and what is permissible in general, the laws of Shabbat and Holiday observance, and the laws of family purity, which regulate (sexual) behavior between husband and wife. It is often said that one who follows these three can be counted upon to do the rest of the *mitzvot*. Another source says that wearing *tziztis* daily, the ritual fringes as a visual reminder of the *mitzvot* mentioned in Deuteronomy 22:12, counts as keeping the whole Torah, because who else but those who take the *mitzvot* seriously would don them each day? It is also argued that the responsibility for following these laws belongs to the woman of a household, including wearing tzitzit. Although in most circles only men wear these, it is the mother who trains her little boy to wear them from the age of three. Until recently, she was the one responsible for the kitchen (*kashrut*) and the house (preparing for Shabbat), and for family purity, which is connected with the menstruation cycle. The woman knows best when her period ends, of course, and when she can resume relations with her husband after counting "seven clean days" and dipping in a *mikvah*, a ritual bath. This has nothing to do with physical cleanliness or impurity, but with the fact that every menstruation is a "missed opportunity" of an ovum to grow into a human being. A menstruation is, if you see it that way, a kind of a death that implies laws of ritual impurity. Resuming relations after dipping into a ritual bath lifts that ritual state connected with death into one of life and the happiness of a new honeymoon, every month again. This is why women are revered for the central part they play in maintaining home and family life. And it's also why maintaining *Shalom Bayit*, or peace in the home, is more the responsibility of the husband than it is the wife's. Those ancient rabbis seemed to know what today is still sage advice: Happy wife, happy life.

Essentially, in Judaism the decisions about how we should live our lives are not taken lightly. Inherent in the notion of learning Torah as a blueprint for governing one's life is the principle that we should act not out of our impulses or selfish desires, as might come naturally to human beings. Instead, we should heed the lessons emphasizing sensitivity to others and promoting social justice, a critically important tenet in Judaism. These must be learned because they are contrary to human nature and must come from our intellect instead of our hearts. Once we've engaged our brains, we get to think about what is right or wrong and decide how we will act. In ancient days, it was easy to closely follow Torah teachings. Even today those living in Orthodox communities find it a good deal easier to be traditionally observant compared with their assimilated neighbors. As we noted in the Introduction, it is not easy to be authentically Jewish in a modern world. If one is Ultra-Orthodox it is easy to rigidly follow the rules. Similarly, if one is non-religious it is easy to dismiss the rules and do as you please. But when one wants to live Jewishly in the modern world there are many compromises and decisions that must be made. For example, just getting two *challah* loaves, the *kosher*, braided Shabbat bread, to make the *motzei* (the blessing over bread) and *kosher* wine on Friday evening can present a challenge, unless you live in a city with a large Jewish population where there are *kosher* bakeries, like New York. There are a set of rules governing its preparation that can make the bread fit for every Jew or can invalidate its use except by those who are very assimilated.

Once, one of Bruce's conversion students asked if it was acceptable to pursue a hobby on Shabbat because it involved engaging in an activity that he did not normally do during the week, and therefore honored the Almighty by doing something pleasurable. There is no simple answer to this question, because we are all on different paths of life. In fact, it raises more questions. Does the hobby involve any of the 39 Shabbat prohibitions, the types of

work that are forbidden to perform on Shabbat because they were connected to building the Temple and because they imply making changes from one situation of a certain material into another, which include activities like writing, cutting, sewing, building, or gluing? What is your level of observance? How important is it for you to follow the laws of Shabbat? Most importantly, what is the thought process that may lead to the conclusion that this activity is something that could or should (not) be done? It is very important for (prospective) converts and other Jews to study the laws of *kashrut,* Shabbat, and family purity with great zeal so they can make informed decisions about how best to live Jewish lives.

18. Do I have to go to Synagogue Services?

As noted above, Judaism is a religion of home and family. But being part of a community is crucial. Life events are celebrated with the community and we pray with the community on Shabbat and other days. Specifically, for men it is important to be part of a community and participate in synagogue life. Certain prayers, such as Mourner's *Kaddish*, and rituals can only be performed in a community. The Torah is only read in the presence of a *minyan*, a community or quorum of minimally ten men over the *Bar Mitzvah* age of thirteen. Conservative and Reform synagogues count women in *minyan* as well. Our sages taught that it is preferable to pray with a *minyan* rather than pray alone. Listening to somebody read from the Torah scroll in a community is a *mitzvah*. It's not the same as reading it from a book at home, which in itself is a praiseworthy habit, of course. Study is encouraged for everybody everywhere, whether one is alone, with only a few, or in a large group. As is stated in *Pirke Avot*: "*When two sit together and words of Torah pass between them, the Divine Presence rests upon them. And even one who sits and occupies himself with the Torah, the Holy One blessed be he, appoints him a reward.*"

Being part of a *minyan* when someone needs to say Kaddish for a deceased relative is a *mitzvah*, as well as a good deed (*ma'aseh tov*). The Talmud asks who should attend a *minyan*? The answer is: ten unoccupied men. It says men and not women, because women are exempt from any time-limited *mitzvah*. Prayer Services for morning, afternoon, or evening must occur at fixed times of the day, so women, who have other, more important responsibilities for the family—young children, for instance—are not obligated to attend, although they may if they wish. If someone is occupied by some useful enterprise such as engaging in a trade for example, he is not always obligated to join a *minyan*. Otherwise, it is a good thing to do, but it is more of a moral obligation than a legal one. For a convert, there is the additional benefit to get to know other Jews in the synagogue and invite them, or be invited, for Shabbat meals, participate in community activities, and learn while having a good time. Most rabbis will reject a prospective convert if s/he is not able, or worse, not willing, to participate in Synagogue Services regularly.

Most assimilated Jews only participate in Worship Services for the High Holy Days, (Yom Kippur and the Jewish New year, Rosh Hashannah) and some of the fun holidays, like Simchat Torah and Purim, as well as when attending a *Bar* or *Bat Mitzvah* celebration. Naturally, this has created some difficulties for Jewish communities. Because attendance in a neighborhood with many assimilated Jews is rare, or sporadic at best, synagogues have been experiencing financial crises with some having to close their doors or merge with other synagogues. In some areas, scarcely more than 10% of the Jewish population is affiliated with congregations. One recent study found that the only congregations that were thriving were for a greater part Chabad centers, representing the Ultra-Orthodox branch of Judaism. This represents a problem for those wishing to convert or join a congregation once conversion has been completed. The Ultra-Orthodox hold to the stringent rules of traditional Judaism. Unless an Orthodox conversion was completed, the convert–or the non-Jewish spouse of someone born Jewish—will never be fully accepted. This is true even if the prospective convert is devout and thoroughly observant–perhaps even more observant than those who are Jewish by birth. Moreover, those wishing to participate in a Modern Orthodox, Conservative, or even Reform community options will be diminished in the future. We are simply offering an observation and not offering any solution to what may become a significant issue among Jews, which is the changing face of the Jewish population. At the current rate, in fifty years the modal Jewish person in the United States will very likely be someone who identifies as a member of Chabad or another (Ultra-)Orthodox sect. And while we believe congregations should educate their members on the importance of attending synagogue services regularly, individuals are the ones who make the ultimate decision regarding the benefits of attendance.

19. Do I have to learn Hebrew?

Learning to read at least some Hebrew is a requirement. Hebrew is the language of the Torah that has kept the Jews together over millennia and during our dispersion over the whole world. It is the glue that keeps us united. Shoshannah once visited a Bukharian synagogue in Jerusalem. She could follow the service perfectly, only because it was in Hebrew. What if we were to use the language of the country where we live? Would that not exclude our fellow Jews to a great extent? The convert does not have to become an expert, but must know enough Hebrew to follow the service in the synagogue and say blessings and Shabbat prayers. Our sages taught that Hebrew is the language of G-d, who spoke holy words of Hebrew and the world came into existence. Consequently, Hebrew is the holy tongue, or *Lashon Kodesh*. But in the time of the Talmud, people in Israel generally spoke Aramaic, no longer Hebrew. Hebrew was reserved for scholars, holy writings, and prayers. In those days most people could not read Hebrew well enough, let alone understand it well, requiring the prayer leaders to read in their stead. It was then that people started to translate biblical texts, for instance into Aramaic, but also into Greek or Latin, and later in many other languages as well. But we all know that translations cannot be one hundred percent accurate and diminish the essence of the Hebrew text—or any text. Therefore, we strive to read texts in the original language, Hebrew, as much as possible and use translations only to assist us, depending, of course, on the level of knowledge of the reader. Modern Hebrew is spoken in Israel today, but in other parts of the world not so much. Hebrew remains the holy language and prayers in Synagogue Services continue to be read in Hebrew, although many Progressive congregations intersperse the native language with Hebrew during the Prayer Service. While it is believed that G-d hears our prayers irrespective of the language we use, reading Hebrew allows us to be more connected with our heritage and the generations that came before us. For that reason, it should be required that all Jews become familiar with Hebrew and develop the ability to at least read some prayers, even if it is just a little. The single prayer that most Jews can chant in Hebrew is the first line of the *Shema: Shema Yisroel, Adonai Eloheinu, Adonai echad*. In English it is: *Hear O Israel, the L-rd our G-d, the L-rd is one*.

20. What goes on during a Jewish Religious Service?

A religious service–typically a Shabbat Service—in a synagogue follows an order that is laid out in the *siddur*, or prayer book. The Morning Service, called *Shacharit*, begins with introductory communal prayers. In most rites these include the Thirteen Articles of Faith written by one of the most important Jewish scholars, the medieval Rabbi Moshe ben Maimon, aka Maimonides (in an acronym: Rambam; see Question #3). It is followed by Psalms and other Biblical, Talmudic and medieval texts. Some prayers are said softly and privately, some are read aloud or chanted by the prayer leader, and some are read or chanted in unison or alternately by the cantor and the congregation.

Two very important prayers are the *Shema Yisrael* and the *Amidah*. *Shema Yisrael* is the quintessential Jewish expression of faith: *Hear, oh Israel, the Eternal is our G-d, the Eternal is One* (Deuteronomy 6:4). It is followed by more Torah texts and by the *Amidah*, literally, the *Standing Prayer*, because it is recited silently while standing solemnly with one's feet close together, and later repeated out loud by the cantor. This prayer is also called the Silent Prayer or the Eighteen Benedictions. In reality there are nineteen, but one of them was aimed against heretics—specifically the new Christian sect that was considered a threat to Judaism in the time of the Talmud,—and has been forbidden by different non-Jewish rulers in different times, assuming that this benediction was aimed against them. And in some cases they were right. The *Amidah* contains important tenets of Judaism, mentions what G-d has done for us, and gives praise and thanks to Him.

These prayers are followed by a ritual wherein one or more handwritten parchment Torah scrolls are removed from the ark, the *Aron Kodesh* or Torah shrine, followed by the Torah reading, which, as has been described above—is chanted according to a specific melody or trope. This is called *leyning* in Yiddish. Chassidim, Ashkenazim and Sephardim each have their own style of trope. *Leyning* is immediately followed by chanting a portion from the Prophets or other books in Tenakh. This non-Torah text is called the Haftarah. The scroll(s)—on some days we read from more than one scroll—are then returned to the ark with a brief ceremony accompanied by chanting some prayers. The rabbi, prayer leader, or member of the congregation then offers some commentary about the Torah reading, called a *dvar* (literally a word, meaning words and explications of the Torah and religious law). There may instead be a sermon that relates to an aspect of the Torah reading, or some significant social event. The service continues often with a healing prayer for the sick, known as a *mishebeyrac*h, and a prayer in remembrance of the deceased, known as Mourner's *Kaddish*, which requires a quorum of ten men in Orthodox circles or ten people in non-Orthodox circles, also referred to as a *minyan*. If the service is for observance of a *Bar* or *Bat Mitzvah*, there will also be some recognition of this, including introduction of the tallit (in some circles) and blessing given by the officiant. There may also be a series of speeches, including those made by the *Bar* or *Bat Mitzvah*, parents, and perhaps synagogue dignitaries. In an Orthodox *shul* and a Conservative synagogue, the Morning Service is followed by *Mussaf*, literally the Additional Service, which contains an *Amidah* as well. This is in commemoration of certain additional sacrifices for Shabbat and holidays in the Temple in Jerusalem in biblical times. After a *Bar/Bat Mitzvah* there is usually a festive meal called a S*e'udat Mitzvah*. If there is no *Bar* or *Bat Mitzvah* there is often a *kiddush*, starting with the mandatory blessing over a cup of wine by the rabbi or somebody who gets the honor, followed by food, or at least coffee and cake, and socializing.

There is an Afternoon Service called *Minchah* (after the afternoon sacrifice in the Temple in Jerusalem), which features of course the silent *Amidah*. It is often followed directly by the Evening Service, called *Maariv* (in Sephardic circles *Arvit*), with the *Shema* and *Amidah* as the most important prayers. Orthodox men attend Synagogue (or *Shul)* Services at least twice a day, also during the week, or gather with other Jews for a (private) *minyan* (in Yiddish also called *minya),* a quorum of ten adult Jewish males. They have *minyan*im before and after work and in companies with many Jewish employees sometimes at work, in an office. Weekday prayers are shorter and take less time than the longer Shabbat Service. In Orthodox and Conservative synagogues, the Torah is read not only on Shabbat, but on Monday and Thursday as well.

21. Do Jews read the Bible in Temple or Synagogue?

"Temple" is the term used for a synagogue of the Reform movement, everybody else says synagogue. The word synagogue comes from Greek and means a place to come together, the same as the Hebrew *beit knesset*, a "house to come together." In Orthodox circles, the Yiddish word *shul*, which refers to the synagogue as a place for both prayer and study is used. *Shul* shares the same etymological root as school. Learning or studying is one of the pillars of Judaism.

During Worship Service we use a prayer book called a *siddur*. People may bring their own personal prayerbook or borrow one from the bookshelves in the Synagoge. The *siddur* sets out the order of the *nusach*, the liturgy. Different branches of Judaism use different *siddurim*, which follow either an Ashkenazy or Sephardic tradition, but they all follow more or less the same elements and order. It is interesting that Chassidim, who are for the overwhelming majority Ashkenazim, use a Sephardic *siddur*. The reason for this is that they honor and follow a great medieval Sephardic kabbalist, Isaac Luria, who lived in Tzfat. *Siddurim* and *machzorim*, the prayerbooks for holidays, are used as a guide for the Prayer Service. Excerpts from Torah and other biblical writings, such as Psalms, are contained in prayers. On Shabbat and other holidays sections from the Torah are read, depending upon where the date falls on the Jewish calendar. It must be noted that what the Christians call the Bible is for them both the Old and New Testament. Jews only have the "Old Testament," which they don't call that name, of course, but *TeNaKH*, an acronym for *Torah*, *Neviim* and *Ketuvim*, the Torah, the Prophets and the Scriptures (i.e., all other books, such as Psalms and Proverbs). The Torah, which contains the Five Books of Moses, is the most important. The Torah reading from a special parchment scroll in the synagogue is followed by selections from the Prophets and other biblical Books (read from a book, not from a scroll) that are thematically related to the Torah reading. Worshippers read along from their *Chumash*, a book containing the weekly Torah portions and related texts from the Prophets and other Scriptures. These have been determined and follow a certain order, rather than left to the discretion of the rabbi at any given synagogue.

The Torah has been divided into equal portions for the approximately fifty Shabbatot (plural of Shabbat) of the Jewish lunar year, which has 353, 354, or 355 days; however, in Talmudic times some congregations followed a three-year Torah reading cycle. It contains several leap years with an additional month during a cycle of nineteen years in order to have Festivals occur in their due season. Many Biblical Festivals have agricultural origins and the harvest Festival must not occur in winter, of course. On Simchat Torah, occurring a few

weeks after the autumnal New Year, Rosh Hashannah, the old cycle of Torah portions is completed with the last verse of Deuteronomy and we begin the new cycle, starting with Genesis. All the Torah scrolls the synagogue owns, which are usually at least two but often some more, are taken out of the *aron*, the shrine where they are kept. The whole community dances around with them in between finishing the concluding portion and beginning with the first portion. The large and precious parchment scrolls have been hand written by a trained scribe called a *sofer*. It is placed on a special lectern called the *beemah* (also spelled as *bimah*). Seven people are called up successively to make a blessing, a *berakhah*, before the *baal koriah,* also called *baal kore*, the "reader," chants the seven parts of the weekly *parshah* (portion) from the unvocalized text from the scroll. This *baal kore* might be a rabbi or cantor, or someone trained in the trope and reading unvocalized Hebrew texts. It takes a lot of training to do it correctly. A *Bar* or *Bat Mitzvah* usually learns to cantillate (part of) his/her weekly portion with a special tutor. Many students train so long and hard that they still know that part by heart when they are older. A *baal kore* is held in high esteem and is indispensable for a Jewish community.

22. Why is there Antisemitism?

This is a good question. Unfortunately, we do not have a definitive answer because it is extremely complicated. Theories abound attempting to explain this very old question. For centuries, Christians have been taught that "the Jews killed Jesus." In combination with economic envy this has created an undercurrent of subtle Antisemitism still festering in the Western World. Rather than delineate the various explanations that have been suggested, we suggest you research this topic for yourself and find an explanation that resonates with you. Suffice it to say that none of the reasons people may have for their Antisemitism are based on sound reasoning. Nor do they reflect desirable moral or character qualities. Antisemitism has been around for millennia and will likely continue because it is irrational and represents baseless hatred. Jews have been and continue to be a minority in most countries. Successful Jews evoke envy from unsuccessful non-Jews (and from unsuccessful Jews as well, but they usually don't become antisemites) Jews wishing to stay within their own community and their own religious environment, eating strictly kosher and marrying only Jews, evoke a "do they think they are better than us?" reaction. Typically, Jews being barred from most professions in history and forced into moneylending are seen as bloodsucking moneylenders. A Dutch saying goes that whoever wishes to hit a dog will find a stick.

Shortly after Donald Trump was elected President of the United States, there was an uptick of Antisemitism and hate crimes toward Jews, as well as toward LGBTQ (lesbians, gays, bisexuals, transsexuals, queer people), People of Color, and Muslims. Why this happened remains a mystery to some, but many suggest that it has something to do with the ultra-nationalistic and patriotic approach of White nationals towards the perceived "strangers." i.e. the immigrants or foreigners. Jews are ideal scapegoats in the eyes of some. Most American Jews are not immigrants, as they have lived in this country for generations just like their Christian counterparts. In the seventeenth century, when New York was still a Dutch colony and called New Amsterdam, it had a considerable number of Jewish inhabitants. Most paid their taxes, obeyed the law, and were therefore accepted as citizens in good standing. Some of their descendants migrated west, others stayed in New York and can be counted among the oldest American families. The biggest group of Jewish immigrants to the United States arrived in the late nineteenth and early twentieth century, mainly from Eastern Europe. Their English-speaking American descendants are for the overwhelming part citizens in good standing.

That is the ironic thing: the First Nation can call themselves the only original Americans, all the others came later and are (the descendants of) immigrants. However, alt-right extremist hate-groups who wish for a homogenous "white and Christian nation" America spew their hatred against everything and everybody who isn't white and Christian like them, including the First Nation. It is especially baffling inasmuch as former President Trump's daughter is a convert to Orthodox Judaism and her Jewish husband was a trusted adviser. Trump's son Eric also got married in 2014 under a *chuppah*, although neither he nor his wife are Jewish. Having Jewish children and grandchildren, Mister Trump had a closer relationship to Jews and Judaism than any previous US president, was a fervent supporter of Israel, as are many fundamental Christians, yet irrational hatred toward Jews continues. Why does this happen? The economy? Did former President Trump, who is lax in reacting to or condemning Alt-right violence, give antisemites the courage to come out of the woodwork? In search of a (nationalistic) anchor in a bewildering and globalizing world, which many consider threatening? Only G-d knows. Brooklyn-born scholar Yossi Klein Halevi, who is a fellow at the Shalom Hartman Institute in Jerusalem and author of *Letters to My Palestinian Neighbor*, was on a book tour and made the following comments:

Antisemitism has always existed and it will always exist. Why? Because. That's why. It just does, regardless of what the Jew does or doesn't do, we are always singled out for hatred. We are always used as the scapegoat. Just check the history books! And every society that goes down the Antisemitism direction always ends up self-destructing. And don't think because things have been so good in America that Antisemitism won't get really bad for us there either. Things were great in Spain, with religious Jews acting as advisors to the Kings and Queens, and then we were expelled. Things were great in Germany and then came the Holocaust. No, I'm not saying that another Holocaust will happen in the US, but life for Jews in American will get more and more uncomfortable and dangerous. Don't delude yourselves in thinking otherwise. Just as Jews in England were safe a decade ago, look at what is happening there today, with one of the major political parties actually supporting an antisemitic leader, and enabling Antisemitism to grow!

23.   Will I be confronted with antisemitic stereotypes and strange beliefs?

This question is related to the former one, about Antisemitism. The answer is yes, there is a big chance you will be confronted with some weird beliefs that are, unfortunately, going around about Jews relating to how they supposedly look, what they think, and how they supposedly behave. Some of these are based on medieval superstitions that have survived like weeds among less educated people until our day and age. We mention a curious question that has been asked by non-Jewish Americans to their Jewish fellow Americans: "I understand that Jews have horns. Can I see your horns?" So, if I convert to Judaism will I grow horns? No, of course not! We have heard many epithets thrown at Jews reflecting prejudice and hatred and accept them for what they are; unabashed Antisemitism. But the question about Jews having horns is sometimes expressed even by people who are more or less educated and otherwise intelligent, but coming from places where there are few or no Jews. Thus, it appears to be a significant question to address by discussing the origin of the belief.

Dating to the years following the destruction of the second Temple and Roman leader Pompey's military campaign, a diaspora had Jews scattering throughout the world. With it came suspicion and apprehension about Jews that was exacerbated by Christian Church edicts that discouraged social engagement with Jews, because they refused to accept Jesus as their Messiah. Later, to both separate and humiliate Jews, they were ordered to wear special identifiers, such as hats and badges designating them as distinct from Christians. Some of these hats look like a pair of horns.

The foundation of European history parallels the spread of Christianity as a political, military and social force more than simply a theosophy. By the fourth century CE, the Holy Roman Empire reached into Iberia (now Spain and Portugal). Near what is today the city of Grenada, a series of meetings were held between nineteen bishops and twenty-six priests, known as the Council of Elvira during the early part of the century. They created eighty-one canons, none of which had any theological base. Instead, they were aimed at directing and controlling the lives of not only Christians, but of others residing in the realm as well. Jews, along with pagans and heretics, were to be kept from interacting with the Christian population. One of the canons prohibited Jews from marrying Christians or blessing their crops. Another refused communion to any Christian who shared a meal with a Jew. The council also emphasized celibacy for clergy, a reiteration of a canon established in the Council of Antioch (268). There was a great deal of concern over sexual behavior dating to Saint Paul's argument that celibacy was the best way to become ready for the kingdom of

Heaven. This was consistent with a view that marriage was undesirable since it promoted conflict between people, suffering, and sin. The Jewish view is quite the opposite. Marriage is seen as a natural and desirable state of affairs in which the souls of the husband and wife are completed as the Divine Presence comes to rest over the marriage at the time they are joined, which is termed Kiddushin, reflecting the holiness of the event.

The next two centuries witnessed the Church's efforts to assert themselves further into Jewish life. In the year 613 in Iberia, under King Toledo III, Jews were ordered to convert to Christianity or face expulsion. Many Jews left, but others continued as crypto-Jews who publicly acknowledged themselves to be Christian but practiced Judaism secretly. Twenty years later, in 633, the fourth Council of Toledo convened to address the problem of crypto-Jews and Marranos. The Council decided that if professed Christians were determined to be secretly practicing Judaism their children would be taken from them and raised in monasteries or proper Christian homes.

Sometime during the 12th century, the notion that Jews cavorted with Satan who gave them magical powers became popular among Christians. Antisemitic sentiment existed for centuries in Christian culture as Jews were considered the killers of Christ. Blaming Jews for the death of Jesus, himself a Jew who taught lessons containing basic Judaism, seems odd to us, since if he had not died through crucifixion at the time he did, there would have been no salvation for Christians and no Christianity. If Jews cavorted with the devil, Satan, who is depicted as horned and having goat feet, would it be possible that Jews have horns as well? And therefore, in some places Jews were forced to wear two-pointed hats resembling big horns.

However, this should not be mixed up with an other story about "Jewish horns" that is based on an error in translation. In Exodus 34:29 Moses descends Mount Sinai with the Tablets of the Law and his face exudes "rays of light," he is beaming. The Hebrew word for ray, *qeren*, has been translated by Saint Jerome in his fourth century Latin Vulgata Bible translation as *cornu*, which sounds very similar but primarily means "horn." Based on this misunderstanding, artists and Bible illustrators have depicted Moses—the Jew par excellence, representing the Old Testament with this Tablets of the Law—as bearing horns on his head. A famous example is the large horned Moses statue of Michelangelo Buonarroti. At the time of Saint Jerome, Antisemitism was already widespread and has likely influenced his writings, for example his statement that anyone making false interpretations of scripture "Belongs to the synagogue (sic!) of the Antichrist."

The assumption was not challenged and became part of the lore associated with Jews. Jews no more have horns than do Christians, Moslems, or any other people. Someone converting to Judaism will not grow horns.

24. Will people hate me if I become Jewish? How do I deal with Antisemitism after I convert?

Perhaps we will never fully understand why, but there is quite a bit of anti-Jewish sentiment in the world. Is it jealousy, religious intolerance, imagined or real economic, intellectual, or other envy, an innate hatred against "the other," newcomers or minorities, even if these "newcomers" have lived for hundreds or more than a thousand years in a certain place, like the Polish Jews in Poland and the German Jews in the German Rhineland communities? For centuries, Christians in Europe believed that Jews, having already received the "Old Testament" that includes the Torah, should accept the New Testament as well and become Christians. And if not, they should be persecuted and be subject to Eternal punishment. This has been going on for millennia, and while we don't fancy ourselves pessimists, in all likelihood this kind of ideological Antisemitism will continue indefinitely. Another factor that has caused hatred by non-Jews is the exclusivity of the Jewish religion. Many of us kept and keep *kosher*, certainly in history, which generally interferes with socializing with people who don't keep *kosher*, like non-Jews. The Torah forbids us specifically to intermarry with non-Jews or even participate in their social celebrations, because that might lead to romantic ties that result in intermarriage. To attend their religious festivals is equally taboo. This was a very important prohibition until not so long ago. Now secularism is on the rise among Jews, but for centuries people were steeped in their respective religions which put a heavy stamp on their everyday life and behavior and even objects. Think of fields blessed by a priest and sprinkled with holy water, for instance. We are actually bidden to stay away from other people except for superficial and necessary contacts, like doing business. In many cases a convert to Judaism wasn't (and won't) be looked upon favorably by his or her former coreligionists who, for instance, consider the "renegade" being eternally damned, ungratefully throwing away their Christian salvation and entrance to Christian Heaven.

In the Bible, we are called the Chosen People. This, combined with the fact that observant Jews often keep away from socializing with non-Jews, makes us look arrogant in the eyes of many who are "not chosen." It doesn't help to explain what "chosen" means, namely, having been chosen to receive the Torah and to serve as teachers to other nations to bring them the message of the one true G-d, and that this "privilege" does not come with an easy lifestyle, to say the least. In fact, Rava, one of sages in the Talmud (*Shabbat* 88a) argues that it is ultimately up to each of us to embrace Torah and make it our own. Many antisemites won't want to hear that and their resentment lingers, especially if members of the Jewish minority are successful economically, intellectually, and artistically in their country of residence. This means that you actually are at risk of having people despise you simply because you have become Jewish. And you won't get a pass because you are a convert. Your own family and friends might not be happy that you won't eat in their house anymore—or only if you bring your own food and *kosher* utensils, which is even worse—and won't celebrate Christmas or other (semi-)religious family festivals with them. They may ask if their clean and well washed plates and cups are "not good enough" for you and consider you at best stuck up and arrogant, at worst a fanatic or a mental case. Or they may ask, "Can't we just get a rabbi to bless them?"

Indeed, you will be treated by Jew-haters the same way they treat anyone who is Jewish from birth. You might think they are just lacking information, and be tempted to argue with antisemites to persuade them to change their minds. But since the issue is irrational, our advice on the matter comes from an old adage: "Never try to teach a pig to sing, it wastes your time and annoys the pig." For many Jews, Antisemitism is like wearing shoes a size too small. You might be able to live with it but it's never comfortable. One of the questions the *Beit Din* traditionally asks is if the convert knows that the Jews are an often persecuted and threatened minority, and if that deters him or her for their own safety. You don't have to join a group in danger, but if you join us, you will suffer the same as other Jews.

Unfortunately, Jews expect and became somewhat accustomed to Antisemitism. In our time and age in the United States, it isn't always religion based and/or combined with economic envy, but substituted by Antisemitism thinly veiled as a critical attitude condemning the State of Israel such as by supporting the BDS (Boycott, Divest, Sanction) movement. People are, of course, fully entitled to have an opinion about Zionism, the Israeli State, and the situation in the Middle East, also an unfavorable one from Israel's point of view. But we hope they look at the facts before they form their opinion. The line between normal and informed political criticism of the Jewish State and simply blaming "the Jews" (worldwide) is not always clear. Since Jews are dispersed over the world, there are conspiracy-theorists who accuse "the Jews" of plotting to take over and dominate this world. These rambling conspiracy-theories are usually illogical and based on lies and myths, not facts, but there are those who still believe them. One of the most infamous has been described in a fictional book with the title *The Protocols of the Elders of Zion*. It was published in Russia in 1903 and has been translated into many languages since, fueling hatred and unfounded fear. Depending on whom you ask, the woes of the world are the fault of Jewish capitalists, Jewish communists or socialists, Jewish banks, Jewish Zionists, or just "the Jews." There is so-called racial Antisemitism as well, which culminated during the

Third Reich of Nazi Germany in a sinister scheme to kill all the Jews, because they supposedly contaminated the "Northern/Aryan Race." We see that Right Wing and White Supremacist adherents of this kind of racial Antisemitism usually also loath other groups, like African Americans, Asians, Latinos, and Muslims, or simply immigrants. The fact that Jews, certainly in the Western World, appear "white" does not impress them, in their eyes we are "of a different race." We stated above that Jews are a cultural, ethnic, and religious nation and not a race. Jews come in all shades and colors and have mixed with the people surrounding them, for instance, by marrying converts, which is perfectly fine. Jews from Iraq look more like Arabs than Jews in Germany, who are often blue-eyed and blond like non-Jewish Germans.

Some antisemitic attacks are carried out by groups or organizations, Right Wing, extreme Left-Wing, or Islamic terror comes to mind. And there are individuals, the so-called "lone wolves," who carry out attacks on individual (recognizable) Jews, like the unprovoked attacks in Jewish neighborhoods in Brooklyn, Pittsburgh, Florida and New Jersey we saw in 2019. There isn't much we can do to guard against those misguided perpetrators, because we only find out about them after the fact. Many synagogues nowadays are guarded by police keeping an eye out for suspicious individuals. It's unpleasant but necessary.

25. If I convert but stop practicing am I no longer Jewish?

Once you convert it is like you have been Jewish from birth. As we mentioned, being Jewish means having a Jewish soul. In effect, you consolidate your Jewish soul when you convert. In the case that you already had a Jewish soul but you could not prove your Jewishness—for instance because all the Jewish papers of your family were lost in a war—and must convert pro forma in a so-called *safek giyyur* ("doubt-conversion"), your Jewish soul is now out in the open. This is independent of one's level of observance. Like any other Jews, there will likely be times in your life when your participation in Jewish practices, as well as your faith will wax and wane. Even if you were to temporarily stop practicing Judaism and have periods of time when you are unsure of G-d's intentions, love, or perhaps existence, He will be waiting to welcome you back whenever you decide to return.

The State of Israel grants citizenship to all Jews, whether by birth or having undergone a (recognized Orthodox) conversion. However, Jews who willfully adhere to any other, non-Jewish religion forfeit this "Right to Return" and automatic citizenship. There is the famous case of Brother Daniel, a Jew by birth but a Christian monk by choice. He could not obtain citizenship. Atheist Jews who do not adhere to any other religion have no problem, however, acquiring legal citizenship from the State of Israel. The Laws of Return are complicated and there is no room here to go into all the details, but if you want to make *aliyah*, that is to settle in Israel, you need to study this topic meticulously. In any case, it is best to have an Orthodox conversion because non-Orthodox conversions are not recognized in Israel for the sake of acquiring citizenship, or even for marriage, burial in a Jewish graveyard, etc. It's complicated.

26.   What is a *mikvah* and will I have to go in one?

We touched on the subject of the *mikvah* in Question #5, but it is important, so we'll address it here in a little more detail. A *mikvah*, literally a *gathering* (of water), is a special kind of basin or bath used for ritual immersion. There are very complicated and specific laws governing how it is to be built and function. The main quality is that a *mikvah* must contain water that comes from a natural source or a gathering of living water (*mayim chayim*). A bathtub filled from a tap or an outdoor swimming pool filled from the local water supply do not qualify. The *mikvah* is used at times of joy, like preparing for Shabbat, a Holiday (*yom tov* in Hebrew, or *yontif* in Yiddish, both literally meaning "good day") or a joyous celebration (*simchah*). It is also used to aid spiritual healing after an illness or at time of change, such as having contact with a corpse or at the end of the menstrual cycle (*niddah*). A husband and wife are not allowed to have relations until after menstruation is over and seven "clean" or "white" days have been counted, and until the wife immerses in a *mikvah*, going from the ritual status of a menstruant to a non-menstruant. "Clean" in this context has nothing to do with hygiene or—like in some other cultures—the belief that a menstruant woman is "not pure" and must be separated from the community or even abhorred. This makes women feel inferior. The state of a menstruant can be compared with "mourning" the "death," the lost opportunity of an unfertilized ovum to create new life. But the next cycle with a new ovum offers new opportunities. This doesn't mean that a woman is supposed to get pregnant all the time. It just means that the blood of her menstruation can be compared to tears of the womb, which are "wiped away" by immersing in a *mikvah*, followed by reuniting with her husband, which is a source of joy and pleasure. Because she counts seven "clean" or "white" days after the bleeding stops, there is a big chance that she is at the most fertile point of her cycle when she dips in the *mikvah*. The end of the temporary separation every month is like a little honeymoon. In traditional communities, it is essential to have a *mikvah*, because its use is critical to faithful adherence to the laws of family purity for the menstruant woman. Without a *mikvah* she cannot be with her husband and this destroys the *Shalom Bayit*, "peace of the home" in a marriage. So important is having a *mikvah*, that the Sages advised a community to even sell their Torah scrolls—if need be—in order to build a *mikvah*. As Jews move away from traditional practice, unfortunately, the use of *mikvah* has become less significant for many Jews. In Reform Judaism, there is considerably less concern over use of the *mikvah*, as with many other traditional practices.

Immersion symbolizes a dramatically different physical environment compared with air. In water, one can be completely touched by Divinity, since water has long been a representation of divine energy. When one's body is thoroughly surrounded by water, it is as

if G-d is caressing her/him with His love. In traditional circles, ritual immersion (and in addition circumcision for men) is an essential element for a conversion to be completed, the ritual known as the Ceremony of *Tevilah*. For the person who immerses in a *mikvah*, there may not be any barrier or obstacle between the water and one's body. Not only clothes, but all makeup, jewelry, even band-aids are removed. The fillings in one's teeth and other parts that cannot be removed easily or without pain, however, are not considered an "obstacle," but glasses or swimming goggles are. One should completely relax during the immersion, keep one's fingers spread and not in a fist, and even keep one's mouth not completely closed and let the water touch every possible part of one's body. Without immersion in a *mikvah* a conversion would not be complete. Whether or not you will be required to immerse in a *mikvah* at the completion of your conversion is up to your rabbi and the *Beit Din*, who may or may not require it, but most do. Bruce always requires immersion in a *mikvah* for conversion, even if the convert is an infant born to a non-Jewish mother. Most find immersion in a *mikvah* at the time of conversion adds to their spirituality and heightens the experience as it marks a personal changing context into the world of Judaism. They enter the *mikvah* basin as a non-Jew and emerge as a Jew. And often their faces have a radiant glow.

27.   I'm already circumcised. Will I need a *bris*?

This all depends on who is supervising the conversion and the *Beit Din* that will ultimately grant approval. If the conversion is Orthodox, by all means there must be a ritual in which a little blood (a drop) is drawn (*hatafat dam brit*). It must be done by a qualified *mohel* (the specially trained person who performs ritual circumcisions) who is familiar with the laws and rituals, as well as perfected surgical knife skills through considerable supervised practice. Special blessings must be recited. If the conversion is less traditional, it is at the discretion of the *Beit Din* to decide if this is necessary. But it would be highly unusual for the conversion to be completed if the convert were not circumcised, earlier or even right before his conversion, except among the most liberal Reform Jews. To understand why, let's consider the biblical injunction. It is prescribed in the Torah to symbolize the covenant between G-d and Abraham, and it has been performed on male children at the age of eight days for thousands of years. The eighth day is significant, because it is at this age the likelihood of infant mortality diminishes. Also, according to *Gematria* (numerology, the system in which the numerical value of Hebrew letters is used to explain a word, sentence, or idea in the Torah), the number eight represents transcendence. The number seven represents wholeness, like the seven days of the week, the number of times we wrap tefillin around our arms, or the seven levels of Heaven. But, the number eight is an emblem for holiness as it goes beyond the mundane. Here we can think about the number of strands of each corner of a *tallit* (prayer shawl). It was no coincidence that there are eight days of Chanukah, since this festival emphasizes the presence of G-dliness within the miracle of the lights.

Then, in addition to continuing the tradition of the covenant, we also have the Kabbalistic view of circumcision. In brief, the Kabbalistic perspective holds that when G-d —Who is omnipresent— decided to create the physical universe, He contracted into Himself to make room for it. Then there was a great explosion with G-dly sparks flying everywhere ending up in all creations. The outer husk that was unable to contain the massive divine energy is termed *klipah*, which does not allow divine light to pass through. The foreskin contains a high concentration of *klipah* and when it is removed allows holiness to enter the person. With an intact foreskin it is not possible to experience the degree of divine light that is necessary to embody the holiness that befits a Jewish person.

But the main and basic reason that a (ritual) circumcision is required is that a male simply cannot enter the Covenant of Abraham, making him part of the Jewish people, without a *bris*, a ritual circumcision, even if it involves just drawing a drop of blood for an already circumcised male.

Although it is a custom to circumcise babies at the eighth day after birth, circumcision is possible, and even mandatory for Jews if this wasn't done for any reason, medical or otherwise. Many Jews from the former Soviet Union who emigrated to the United States underwent circumcision at an adult age, and celebrated a *Bar Mitzvah* years after the usual age of thirteen. Abraham himself, the "Father of all Jews," was commanded to circumcise himself, his son Ishmael, and all males in his household when he was ninety-nine years old (Genesis 17). Those who are not circumcised (other than for pressing medical reasons) are considered to be spiritually cut off from the Jewish people, as is stated in Genesis 17: 11-14:

You are to undergo circumcision, and it will be the sign of the covenant between Me and you. For the generations to come every male among you who is eight days old must be circumcised, including those born in your household or bought with money from a foreigner—those who are not your offspring. Whether born in your household or bought with your money, they must be circumcised. My covenant in your flesh is to be an everlasting covenant. Any uncircumcised male, who has not been circumcised in the flesh, will be cut off from his people; he has broken my covenant.

There is a spiritual reason for circumcision. The Tanakh speaks on several occasions of a circumcision of the heart, as in Jeremiah 4: 1-4:

If you, Israel, will return, then return to Me, declares the L-rd. If you put your detestable idols out of sight and no longer go astray, and if in a truthful, just and righteous way you swear, 'As surely as the L-rd lives,' then the nations will invoke blessings by Him and in Him they will boast. This is what the L-rd says to the people of Judah and to Jerusalem: Break up your unplowed ground and do not sow among thorns. Circumcise yourselves to the L-rd, circumcise your hearts, you people of Judah and inhabitants of Jerusalem, or my wrath will flare up and burn like fire because of the evil you have done—burn with no one to quench it.

The meaning of this is to make your heart and thoughts holy and dedicated to *HaShem*, G-d, and to Him alone. It is medically impossible to circumcise one's heart, but being physically circumcised is a continual reminder of the spiritual circumcision of the heart we have to perform to honor the covenant with G-d.

28. Can I be part of the Jewish community if I don't convert?

There are limits to how much acceptance you will receive if you do not formally convert. This is not much different from any other (faith) community. Among Christian denominations, if one is Christian but was raised in another denomination, one cannot become a voting member of a congregation until s/he completes some requirements that make them official members. For example, if one was raised Catholic, but later decides to become Lutheran, s/he will not be fully accepted until completion of a brief orientation to Protestant theology, despite being a lifelong follower of Christianity. The rules for conversion to Judaism are typically more stringent. Some Orthodox and Conservative congregations are notoriously unwelcoming to non-Jews, which is for a large part based on many unpleasant experiences in history and ingrained in our perception, such as when an interfaith couple seeks membership. Jewish conversion is supposed to be inspired by a deep longing and desire to join the Jewish people, and not merely by the desire to marry a person who happens to be Jewish. In the latter case, it can be assumed that the person would convert to other religions as well for the sake of their perspective spouse or to please their prospective in-laws. Unfortunately, this is not uncommon. Often, the non-Jewish spouse is marginalized and treated like an interloper. We witnessed this ourselves, and are alternately horrified and saddened by the lack of empathy extended to our fellow humans. We've also seen times when Jews visit synagogues and some members make them feel unwelcome because they are not dues-paying members. This is, of course, both against the spirit of

Judaism and against common human, social decency. One thing that made the Baal Shem Tov and other early chassidic Masters so popular was that many embraced their fellow humans warmly and instilled a love for every creature in their followers. There's a lesson for all of us.

29. Can I keep my Christmas tree when I convert?

In one word, "Yes," says Rabbi Bruce, and in two words, "absolutely not," says Maggidah Shoshannah. In Judaism, people often disagree about important questions and here you get a *forshpays* (Yiddish for starter course, a snack before the main meal). Or, when referring to discussions between Republicans and Democrats, President Gerald Ford once famously quipped, "We can disagree without being disagreeable." Bruce says there is a position that holds if you grew up in a Christian family and participated in holiday celebrations that gave you joy and for which you have fond memories there is no reason why you cannot have reminders of early family life as long as you practice Judaism exclusively. Many of our colleagues would disagree with him, but he believes that since Christmas trees have pagan roots and are not truly religious symbols, in the way a crucifix is, there may be little harm to living a Jewish life.

Shoshannah, however, has the opinion like many other Jews of European descent that it is a sign of utter assimilation which might lead, eventually, to giving up (or watering down to the extent of disappearing) one's Judaism and incorporate other signs of defection from Judaism, such as intermarriage. Since a Christmas tree is a pagan symbol originally used to celebrate the Winter Solstice, and in many verses in the Torah we are strictly forbidden to follow heathen customs, like tattoos, or imitate their rites and festivals, it follows that Jews should not have Christmas trees in their homes. Also, one who converts should not embrace symbols that are associated with one's former faith or non-Jewish lifestyle. Especially not if one converted *out of free will* and openly embraced Judaism. If a convert wants to see a Christmas tree and cherishes childhood memories, s/he can still visit a friend or relative or look at the ubiquitous trees in shop windows or in public displays in the month of December. In the USA, many shops and residential buildings display a *chanukiah* besides a Christmas tree in December and some even include a Kwanzaa candleholder. In Berlin, there are a huge Christmas tree and a *menorah* standing side by side right directly in front of the Brandenburger Gate. But *your* home should proudly display a *chanukiah* in winter. Not a tree.

In the nineteenth and early twentieth century, many German (and some Dutch) Jews had Christmas trees in their houses. They felt fully integrated into society and embraced this ancient Germanic symbol in the knowledge that it was older than Christianity, more folkloric than religious. There is a Christmas tree in the Jewish Museum in Berlin with a sign that says, "What does a Christmas tree do in a Jewish museum?" followed by an explanation about German Jews and assimilation in (pre-war) Germany. But as they found out to their horror, it would not help German Jews to be assimilated. They were made fully aware by Germans of other (or no) faiths of the fact that the Jews are "different." Indeed, we are different! A convert should be well aware of this and take Jewish history into consideration before he or she converts. One can look at the family photos and have fond memories, but once s/he converts, one's behavior should be Jewish while at the same time being respectful of their non-Jewish relatives and their traditions. So, it's preferable to put a Chanukah *menorah* (or a whole collection of them) in your window and view the Christmas tree of the neighbors through their window.

You may have noticed that many modern Jewish families in the US adopted the custom of having Christmas trees in their homes to represent their assimilation into American culture. Both of Bruce's parents had Orthodox upbringings. His uncle married a woman who was raised in a Reform home. He witnessed his first "Chanukah bush" in their home. Bruce thinks that for someone who has converted it is not only a means of rekindling fond memories, but it is also a way of showing respect for one's roots and one's family of origin. In Judaism, we're really big on being respectful to others and not hurting their feelings. Shoshannah agrees on showing respect, but thinks you should not bring Buddha statues or Christmas trees and the like in your home, especially not if they had a religious significance for you and your family before you converted. She noticed an interesting phenomenon when she lived in Berlin. Certain non-Jews (and certainly Germans) are often self-conscious about religious symbols in their own house when a Jew is visiting. A friend asked Shoshannah if he had to remove his Christmas decorations from the table when she stopped by for coffee. No, of course not, it is his house! His nice decorations offended no one. Shoshannah would not remove her *menorah* for visitors either. She had a different but funny experience when she came to America. Not being aware of upcoming Halloween, since that was hardly known and even less celebrated in Holland at the time, she saw a garden full of plastic cobwebs, skulls, plastic gravestones, skeleton hands, and bloody eyeballs. Her first impression was that this must be the house of a deranged psychopath. She absolutely prefers to see a nice Christmas tree, but would not bring one into her home. Our opinion is to respect each other's symbols and decorations and keep your own. That is the Jewish attitude.

30. Why do I need a Jewish name?

In Judaism, a name represents one's inner essence. It is assumed that knowing someone's name means that we know something about a person's character. When we name a child for a relative we are ostensibly saying that we would like for the child to develop the namesake's personality or character traits. In Ashkenazy tradition, babies are not named after living relatives, whereas in Sephardic tradition it is considered an honor to name children for living relatives, such as parents or grandparents. Maggidah Shoshannah had to compromise when her children were born, because in Holland many Ashkenazim follow Sephardic traditions, but her husband of Eastern-European origin does not. So, her daughter was named after her and his deceased (grand-)mother, but her son got as his second given name the second given name of her father, who is still alive, but has a different first given name as her son, and everybody was happy. Since the son was born on Chanukah, his parents picked a first given name related to that Festival. It is also common to name children in honor of biblical figures or religious luminaries. Jewish names state the first (and second) name(s) followed by *ben* for a son or *bat a* for daughter followed by the name of either just the father or father and mother. For converts, it is custom to use the biblical names Avraham and Sarah, because they were the first couple to accept the one G-d, be monotheist in the Jewish sense, and therefore the father and mother of all Jews. So, if you selected the name Moses, your Hebrew name would be Moshe ben Avraham v'Sarah. Many Jews, converts or not, have a name that has a similarity in sound, or bears the same first letter(s), as their "English" name, e.g., Eric and Isaac, Morris and Moses, or their English name is the English version of their Hebrew name (Sarah and Sadie). Shoshannah's European name is Jeanne, which in Holland is pronounced like Shan. In America she only uses her Hebrew name, because Americans pronounce Jeanne as "*Dzheenee*" which reminds her of the Arabic *dzhin* (genie), the kind of spirit dwelling in Aladdin's lamp. Rabbi Bruce's Hebrew name is Dov, and he is named after his maternal grandfather. If you already have a biblical name, let's say, John, which is the English version of Yochanan, what name do you choose then? You can either keep Yochanan, or take a different name if the meaning of the other name or person with that name appeals to you, or for any other good reason. Women converts often choose Ruth, because she was a sincere and praiseworthy convert. Many converts have Jewish ancestors, even if they are remote. Many know this; some do not. You can honor a (great-)great-grandfather, for instance. For this reason, many converts feel they "came home," they are reunited with the tribe they lost in the course of history.

There is another reason to adopt and use one's (new) Hebrew name. In biblical times, the Jews were enslaved in Egypt for 210 years. You can read about this in the Torah in the book of Exodus. But despite the extremely difficult circumstances, they did not assimilate into Egyptian culture. Why is that? Because they kept their Jewish names and customs, like their own clothing style, exactly the same as when they arrived in Egypt. They continued to live as Jewish families, and as a Jewish community. The influence of one's family cannot be underestimated. By using their Hebrew names, converts will feel connected to their new family, which is the whole Jewish community.

Finally, there is a belief that after death people are summoned to the Heavenly Court to account for our lives. First, they are asked for their Hebrew names. But not everybody remembers; it takes getting used to being dead and appearing before the Court. They are confused and may have amnesia for their own names. But every Hebrew name is connected to a biblical verse that starts and ends with the same letters as that name. Many *siddurim*, i.e., prayer books, contain a list of common Hebrew names and the verses they appear connected to. For Shoshannah, it's a verse staring with **Sh** and ending with **h**, which is Psalm 134:2, and for Dov (Bruce's Hebrew name) **D** and **v**, which is Isaiah 55:6. In Orthodox circles, a person quietly recites his or her verse(s), if you have two given names—after the *Amidah* prayer. That helps them to remember.

31.   How will I be tested?

For the most part, once you have completed a program of study and learned whatever your teacher has requested of you, you will be examined by a *Beit Din*, a panel of judges. The questions they ask will come from basic Judaism, history, holidays, and Jewish laws. It is very unusual for anyone to fail, although we've seen a couple of occasions where the candidate was truly ill prepared and had to retake the final interview. Our best suggestion is to wait until you feel you are ready or your teacher tells you that you are ready. Then approach the *Beit Din* with the attitude that no matter what, you cannot fail. If you have taken your studies seriously, absorbed the material and integrated it into your daily life, there can be no such thing as failure. According to the Talmud, the *Beit Din* has to instruct the convert in some easy and some more complicated Jewish laws and customs. But there are no trick questions or pitfalls set up for failure once a candidate is admitted to the *Beit Din*. Shoshannah has acted as a *mikvah* supervisor at several conversions of women, and thus attended their *Beit Din* as well. It was set up in a room in the *mikvah* building and the candidate could immerse immediately after the examination. Some candidates were nervous and just went blank, in which case the rabbis helped them. Insofar as some of the rabbis of the *Beit Din* did not know the candidates personally, they had questioned the teachers of these women—who came from abroad, for instance, from countries that have no *Beit Din* for conversion,— earlier as to how prepared and ready the candidates were. The examination is the last step and means you are in fact already accepted, but it has to be formalized. The glow on the faces of the women emerging from the *mikvah* is something Shoshannah will never forget. She was the first person to see them emerge as Jews and usually offered them a well meant *mazal tov* (congratulations) and the old blessing of our forefathers, which we pronounce on Shabbat evening when we bless our daughters:

May HaShem (G-d) make you like Sarah, Rivkah, Rachel and Leah.
May HaShem bless you and guard you,
May HaShem illuminate His face over you and show you grace,
May HaShem turn His face towards you and make peace for you.

The blessing for a son is similar, but begins with: *May G-d make you like Ephraim and Menasheh.*

This is an interesting blessing. The so-called four Mothers of the Jewish people (the wives of Avraham, Isaac, and Jacob) and the two sons of Joseph, whom we hope our children will emulate, with the help of *HaShem*, had no easy life, on the contrary. They got into all kinds of trouble, they had doubts, argued with G-d, but ultimately, they kept their faith in *HaShem* and were loyal to their people. That is how a Jew should be. Perfection is not required, but trying, and in some cases even struggling, is expected.

32.   What if I change my mind about converting after I've started?

No one will demand that you go through with the conversion process once you begin, or at any time during the process. A decision to convert is a personal choice. There is good reason why converts are officially called "sincere converts," meaning that the only "true converts" are those who convert wholeheartedly and for the sake of Heaven, without ulterior motives. In the time of Mordechai and Esther some people converted out of fear, because they were afraid the Jews might take revenge for Haman's crimes. Or because they considered that the Jews had found favor in the eyes of the king of Persia and would obtain important positions. This is not a good reason to convert, although an understandable one. If you have reasonable doubts that Judaism is the right choice for you, wait, or cancel your plan altogether until you are sure it is the right path for you. The worst thing is that you will have learned something about Judaism. Learning for its own sake is always respected in Jewish culture. We sometimes tell Christians that learning about Judaism can help make them better Christians. If you want to learn about Buddhism or Hinduism because you are interested in knowing about other people and their religions, then by all means go and learn. We are advocates of learning from virtually any source. We know there are Chassidic rabbis who discourage their congregants from reading texts written by non-Orthodox writers out of fear that their understanding of Jewish thought will be watered down. We disagree, and want to encourage exposure to all points of view, including atheists and those who oppose religion. Go ahead and read Stephen Hawking's work and come to your own conclusions. Then read Jewish physicist Gerald Schroeder's work on science and spirituality, or Spinoza. Or the German philosopher Hermann Cohen, who after being an ardent follower of Kantian philosophy returned to the ancient path of his forefathers. Everybody has their own *weltanschauung* (view of of the world) and that view can and often does change. In Judaism we encourage questioning and probing for deeper meaning in order to discover one's own personal truth and path in life. It's not for nothing that one of the most famous Jewish sayings is, Go out and learn!

33. How much will a conversion cost?

Determining the monetary costs is nearly impossible. Each approach to getting the requisite training is established by those who are doing the teaching. In addition to program costs you also have to factor in associated costs such as books and ritual items, including a pair of candlesticks for Shabbat and Holidays, *a tallit* (prayer-shawl), a pair of *tefillin* (phylacteries, which are often expensive), a yearly *lulav* set (a plant bundle for the Festival of Sukkot which is often costly), a *seder* plate (a special plate for the Holiday of Passover), and a Chanukah *menorah* (a candelabra for eight candles), etc. And you have to learn what these are and how to use them properly, of course. Orthodox conversion programs often require that you move to a place with Jewish community, and that you live close enough to a *shul*, or synagogue, to walk there on Shabbat. If you live in Brooklyn there's usually no problem, but if you live in a remote part of a non-Jewish town in, let's say, Kansas, it can become costly and complicated. *Kosher* food, especially *kosher* meat, is generally more expensive than non-*kosher* food, and although you can get the basics nearly anywhere it is challenging to obtain items like Pesach food and *kosher* meat outside of the big Jewish centers. You might have to buy a new wardrobe to become Orthodox. For instance, skinny jeans and tank-tops have to be replaced with stylish but modest dresses, skirts, and blouses. A man, at minimum needs to buy a suit if he doesn't own one to attend *Shul* Services.

Don't forget that nowadays you can gather a lot of knowledge from the Internet, although it is recommended to inquire what sites are legitimate and trustworthy with the aid of a reputable teacher. But to live a Jewish life in a community is different, and an experience you must have. Some people planning to convert follow special courses in Israel, immersing themselves for weeks or months in Jewish life in Jewish towns, but that isn't an option for everybody. On the low end, a conversion in the US might be accomplished for a few hundred dollars and it may range up to a few thousand dollars. Some synagogues do not charge for conversion classes and offer them at no cost as a service to the community as part of their outreach and with the expectation that converts will become dues paying members. Shoshannah has met converts from outside of the US who had to travel to Brooklyn because there was no *Beit Din* for conversion available in their country of origin. Although you can study with a rabbi over the Internet and talk over Skype, for the *Beit Din* it is necessary to meet in person, even if that means that you must spend a considerable amount of money on airfare and a hotel.

34. Why was I turned away when I first inquired about conversion?

Many Christian missionary and outreach programs are designed to bring the Gospel to potential coverts to Christianity and recruit as many new members as possible. We have nothing comparable to this in Judaism. We do, however, have a group called Jews for Judaism that tries to protect Jews from groups that try to convert them to other religions, like Christianity and Islam. There are, for instance, Christian missionary groups active in certain Brooklyn neighborhoods with a large Jewish population from the former Soviet Union. Having grown up in a communist, atheist country, these Russian Jews often do not have enough Jewish knowledge to see through the tricks these missionaries use to snare them, like inviting them for a free "*kiddush*" which turns out to be less authentically Jewish than they think, or offering free food and other help if only people come to their meetings in which they have some Hebrew rituals to make it look "familiar," but they are slipping in a lot of Christian doctrines and beliefs. Some of these missionaries are Jews who have converted to Christianity. Others are non-Jews who studied Judaism, some under the pretext to wish to convert in order to have access to Jewish classes and rabbis. Their goal is not to make better Jews but to make Christians. Shoshannah was once approached by such a missionary in the street in Eilat, in Israel. When he placed himself in front of her and called out, "Jesus saves!" she retorted, "Moses invests," and walked away before he could come up with "an offer she couldn't refuse." Going into discussion with these people is useless.

Dating back to Talmudic times, the rabbis developed a tradition to minimize the conversion to Judaism. There are several legitimate reasons for this. For instance, they were fearful that if it was too easy to become Jewish, Judaism might become watered down by those who did not take the teachings seriously and would bring too many non-Jewish, pagan rituals in their "Jewish" homes. Or who found Judaism fashionable, like the Roman noble ladies who felt drawn to religions that were considered exotic by Romans, like the Persian Mithras cult, the Egyptian cult of Osiris, or... Judaism. They fancied Judaism in a way similar to many people nowadays who love Kabbalah and wear red bracelets and kabbalistic jewelry. Another point to consider is that Jews belonged to an ethnic/cultural/historical tribe, nation, or people, and why would somebody from another "tribe" join them? These people have their own tribe or group they belong to, which has no obligation to live according to often complicated Torah rules as long as they are good and ethical people. Why convert somebody and be responsible as the rabbi who converted her/him for the sins s/he will possibly commit against the Torah and its rules? Another fear was that converts could be disappointed in their new community for any valid or non-valid reason, and turn against that community or the Jews in general. This has happened in history, with disastrous results. Jews were and are a minority in every country except Israel, and we all know how vulnerable minorities are. Combine this with bad old Antisemitism, and you understand why Jews are often cautious to open the door for strangers. Don't forget that by converting to Judaism you don't only "adopt" a religion and lifestyle, but you become a member of the Tribe with its long and complicated history as well. Judaism isn't just a religion, it's a culture and lifestyle based on a people going back thousands of years, guarding and keeping their distinct Jewish identity in every country where the Diaspora has brought them. A French Jew, an American Jew, and a Persian Jew feel connected even though they do not speak the same language or eat the same food, yet all observe the same religious Holidays and pray the same way, some small differences aside.

As a college student, Shoshannah visited Israel and was taken on a tour along different synagogues in Jerusalem during the night of Shavuot, when there are special prayers all night long. As we have mentioned before, she entered a Bukharian synagogue and sat down among women in exotic colorful dresses. They were friendly, but Shoshannah was unable to speak with many of them because they had no language in common. She could follow the *davening* (the prayers), though, because this was all in Hebrew and did not differ much from what she read in her own Ashkenazy *machzor* (prayer book for Holidays) in her native Holland.

Bruce once attended a birthday party for one his son's classmates in elementary school. One of the moms said she converted to Judaism and made the statement "It's easy to be Jewish." His reaction was that she somehow must not really know what it means to be Jewish, because "easy" is not a word Jews use to describe the experience. A famous and often used Yiddish proverb is, "*Es iz shver tzu zayn a Yid,*" (It is hard to be a Jew). And then one sighs.

A custom was born and included in the Talmud (*Yevamot* 47a) that if someone wanted to become Jewish s/he had to ask/beg three times before being accepted. Three symbolizes the establishment of a pattern in Judaism. A cord consisting of three strands isn't easily broken (Ecclesiastes/Koheleth 4:12). If someone asked three times and kept coming back despite being rejected it was considered to be a sincere interest. In many circles this custom exists today.

There is also a small movement to actively recruit converts to Judaism, but it has not gained much traction. And of course, we see fervent efforts by the Ultra-Orthodox Lubavitcher movement (aka Chabad) to find non-practicing or highly assimilated Jews to

bring them back or "convert" them to Ultra-Orthodox Judaism. They have achieved a measure of success. But this is not a real conversion, of course, because everybody involved is already Jewish and this is simply bringing people back into the fold.

35. Will I be accepted in the Jewish World if I convert?

By now, you probably have an understanding that things in Judaism are not so easily divided into black and white. Many times, the answer to the question depends not only on whom you ask, but who's doing the asking. Once, in an Orthodox community day school, the children would ask the rabbi if certain food items were permissible. Yossi asked the rabbi if he could have a certain candy. The rabbi said no. "But rabbi," Yossi protested, "you just told Chaim it was allowed." The rabbi replied, "Yes, I know. You see, his parents are more permissive. I know your parents, and I can guarantee that they would not permit you to eat this candy." Does that mean that something can be *kosher* and not *kosher* at the same time? No, something is *kosher* or it isn't. It means that some people make a protective wall around the minimal standards of *kashrut,* the laws of *kosher*, while others do not, or their wall is lower. For example, some strictly Orthodox people only drink milk from a farm/processing facility with rabbinical supervision. This milk is referred to as *chalav Yisroel* and this is explicitly stated on the package. Others drink milk from a general American farm/processing facility and trust that the food laws in the US are so strict and hygienic that their milk has not been adulterated or been in contact with equipment containing something non-*kosher*. You can ask ten Jews about this and you get at least twelve opinions.

It's the same thing with Jewish conversion. An Orthodox rabbi would only recognize a conversion that was done by someone he knows is also Orthodox. If you want to become part of an Orthodox community you must have an Orthodox conversion. If you do, your conversion will be recognized and you will be universally accepted by all other branches of Judaism. The exception is if you plan to go to Israel and make *aliyah*. In that case, you must go through a conversion by those rabbis who are accepted in Israel as having the authority to grant conversions along with the rest of the *Beit Din*. Just being Orthodox is not sufficient, because in Israel they have their own complex rules. In other words, it has political overtones, which we believe detracts from the spirituality of Jewish life. But it is what it is.

Does that mean that any other conversion is worthless and should be avoided? Of course not. Your reasons for converting and how you plan on living a Jewish life are most important. Virtually any conversion you go through will allow you to affiliate with most mainstream congregations. It's not likely anyone will check to verify how you converted and if the rabbi or *Beit Din* are acceptable, at least outside of the Orthodox community. We've seen some of these rabbis marginalize those who attend their congregations as interlopers and made to feel unwelcome. We have trouble with this kind of treatment of others, because it is far from heeding the admonition to love our neighbors as ourselves.

On the other hand, if you don't honor the rules of the club—any given club—it's not unexpected that you cannot join that club. If you want to join an Orthodox congregation you will have to have an Orthodox conversion. The reason for being standoffish is based on a long history of people who were "interested" but lost interest and even became hostile and caused a lot of trouble for the Jews with their "inside knowledge." In Europe, where Jewish communities not only were decimated by the war but in many cases still have to deal with significant Antisemitism, it is understandable that they are wary of newcomers, especially if these newcomers aren't "members of the Tribe." By converting, you make the commitment to belong. By not converting, you will be seen as a friend by some and as an unwelcome guest by others. It basically depends on who you are, how you act, what you want, and where you are. It is true that there are some people in Jewish communities who still won't accept you completely even if you have a recognized conversion. These individuals are usually not very educated and their bias is based on ignorance, a bad experience, and/or simply a wrong attitude. The Torah commands us to love the stranger who comes to you and after the stranger became a member of the Tribe there is no difference between him or her and a person born Jewish; there is one law for all. This is embodied in the biblical story of Ruth, read during the celebration of Shavuot, which commemorates the giving of the Torah at Mount Sinai. It's also expressed in the laws for Pesach. A "stranger," read: a non-Jew, cannot partake of the *seder* meal or eating from the Pesach lamb in biblical times, but a convert is obligated to eat the lamb (in biblical times, we no longer have a Pesach lamb after the Temple was destroyed) and nowadays, to celebrate the seder like any born Jew.

36. Will my children be Jewish?

If you are a woman and complete your conversion prior to giving birth, your children automatically will be Jewish. If you are male, but the birth mother is not Jewish there will be controversy surrounding the child's authenticity as a Jew in most circles. If you follow a modern, Reform view, if one parent is Jewish and you raise the child as Jewish, then the child is considered Jewish. If you follow a less lenient practice, then it will be necessary for the child to go through a conversion also. For infants it is relatively easy. By the end of the first year of life a ceremony of *Tevilah* ("dipping") is performed in which the child is ritually immersed in a *mikvah* and the parents sign a document pledging to raise the child as Jewish. Bruce has performed a number of these ceremonies. Since he lives near the Florida coast, these ceremonies are completed at the beach where the ocean serves as a *mikvah*, a ritual bath. The requirement for the *mikvah* is that its water come from a natural source and be free flowing. If you have children already and then convert, the children are not considered Jewish and must go through their own conversion. As stated above, an Orthodox conversion is universally accepted. If a child was converted in any other manner and later wants to marry in a universally accepted Jewish ceremony (i.e., Orthodox), or move to Israel, a second, Orthodox conversion will be necessary. This can be emotionally painful. You feel Jewish and live a Jewish lifestyle, but you are not recognized as a Jew. There are known cases of women who had Reform conversions in prewar Germany. Their (great-)grandchildren in the maternal line became *ba'aley teshuvah,* meaning people coming from a non-or not very religious home, or not Orthodox, in any case, who chose to adopt a strict Orthodox lifestyle. They wanted to marry in Israel or marry an Orthodox spouse and looked into their family history—which often yielded ancestors who were rabbis, cantors or Holocaust victims—but could not come up with the right Orthodox papers proving their Orthodox ancestry, like an Orthodox *ketubah*, or wedding contract, from the US or Europe. They were considered "non-Jews" despite having grown up in a Conservative or Reform Jewish family, and were required to go through an Orthodox conversion. For many of these children this is problematic, given the fact that an Orthodox conversion (in Israel and elsewhere) requires the promise to live a traditionally Jewish Orthodox lifestyle, which they weren't accustomed to. Some actually want to live a strict lifestyle but others don't, they just want to have a normal Jewish wedding in Israel. That, and the fact that they are all of a sudden not considered Jewish causes tremendous emotional distress.

Whether you are Jewish by birth or have already converted, when you adopt a child even as a newborn the child will have to go through a conversion. But if the birth mother was Jewish, the child is considered Jewish and will be exempt from completing a formal conversion.

37. What are Jewish lifecycle events?

There are times throughout life that communities come together for celebration, observance, or emotional support. Over the lifetime of Jewish people these include birth, *Brit Milah, the* circumcision and naming for boys, the birth and naming of a girl, *Pidyon ha-ben*, a ceremonial redeeming for first born boys, based on a biblical ritual, *Bar* or *Bat Mitzvah*, coming of age in the religious sense at age thirteen for boys and twelve for girls, called confirmation among members of Reform congregations, marriage (engagement and wedding), and death (attending both funeral and *shiva, the house of mourning*). Members of the Jewish community are invited to participate in all of these transitions in life to share the joy, as when attending a wedding, as well as the sorrow, as we experience during a funeral. Attending weddings and funerals are both *mitzvot*. In other words, they are divine commandments and not simply suggestions. As we've said, it is hard to live a Jewish life without a community, because the community is involved in so many aspects. For many lifecycle events a community of at least a *minyan*, a quorum of ten Jews, is required. Although there were some individuals with the secluded lifestyle of a hermit also in Jewish history, this is not encouraged. Ideally, Jews live in a community of other Jews to support them in times of joy and sadness and to celebrate their festivals with, like Shabbat. During the Covid-19 pandemic, many elderly people were compelled to stay home. They were isolated even during family festivals par excellence, like the *seder* nights of Passover. The community went to great lengths to make sure these isolated individuals not only have everything they needed for the Festival, but stayed in touch via telephone, social media, etc. A Jew can be home alone but should not *be* alone. During that pandemic, there were funerals for those who succumbed to the disease, but only very few people were allowed to attend out of fear of spreading the disease when a crowd gathers. At the ceremony for Shoshannah's father—who died of old age, not Covid—there were only 14 people present. This is against the grain of Jewish customs and emotions and was very hard on families and communities alike. But in this case *not* performing the *mitzvah* of attending a funeral implies the greater *mitzvah* of keeping people safe during a pandemic.

38.   Will I have a *Bar* or *Bat Mitzvah*?

When Bruce turned 63, he decided to have a *Bar Mitzvah Sheini*, a *second Bar Mitzvah* wherein he read from the Torah, chanted the Haftorah (a part from the Prophets or Scriptures connected to the weekly Torah portion), and gave a *dvar* Torah, a lecture about the Torah. But being *Bar* or *Bat Mitzvah* is automatic when one reaches a certain age, thirteen for boys and twelve for girls. Getting called up to the Torah to read is just (very meaningful) window dressing, because the truth is one does not have to do anything or undergo any ritual

to be a *Bar* or *Bat Mitzvah*. Since it is a rite of passage for those who become adults in the religious sense, meaning they are now responsible for doing *mitzvot* and keeping the precepts of the Torah, we like to have a religious celebration and a festive meal, or *Se'udat Mitzvah*. Shoshannah's relatives in Europe who turned thirteen during the Second World War had no ceremony, for sad but understandable reasons. Still, they are all considered *Bar* or *Bat Mitzvah* since they are now over the age of twelve/thirteen. It means that as an adult one can be counted in a *minyan*, a quorum of ten required for certain prayers. It also means that the parents are no longer accountable for any religious sins of the child. Prior to this time, if a child sinned, the parents were held accountable in the Heavenly Court. So now that parents are off the hook, we can see why they would want to spring for a party for the *Bar* or *Bat Mitzvah*. However, the obligation to raise and support their children does not stop at *Bar* or *Bat Mitzvah*, of course. For instance, there was a wide spread custom among Eastern European Jews, especially for the parents of a *kallah* (a bride) to support their daughter and son-in-law as a newly married couple for several years in order to give the often very young husband an opportunity to study Torah in a *yeshivah* (Talmud academy), unburdened by financial responsibilities for his small but hopefully growing family, and later on to set up a business or trade to support for his family. It speaks for itself that the couple was older than *Bar* or *Bat Mitzvah* age.

But completing conversion is certainly a time to celebrate and an occasion to be marked. Something akin to a *Bar Mitzvah* celebration is in order. Some kind of ceremony acknowledging this accomplishment can be arranged. If you complete conversion with a group at a Reform synagogue there will be an official ceremony. This will most likely occur at a Friday Evening Service followed by an *Oneg Shabbat*, which means "delight of the Sabbath," and typically involves some food and baked goods. If you are not part of a group, you can arrange your own celebration. And if you want a belated *Bar* or *Bat Mitzvah*, that's possible. With an online date converter you can calculate your date of birth according to the Jewish calendar and ask your synagogue if they would let you have a *Bar/Bat Mitzvah*. Older people who for whatever reason had no Bar/*Bat Mitzvah* ceremony have done this, for instance those from the former Soviet Union or Holocaust survivors. We also see women who were raised in observant families and had little celebration of their own *Bat Mitzvah* insist on a bigger celebration years later. In some synagogues a *Bat Mitzvah* girl publicly lights candles on the Friday evening following her *Bat Mitzva*h. Every community and every family has their own preferences, or customs. A custom is referred to as a *minhag*.

39.   Why do I have to do more than people who are Jewish by birth?

If one is born Jewish there are no requirements for practice. We take it for granted that someone who is born to Jewish parents is automatically Jewish and despite little or no practice of Judaism in her/his life, or blatantly breaks Jewish laws, is just as Jewish as any other Jew. In other words, someone who eats pork, drives on Shabbat, never attends Worship Services, or does not even believe in G-d is equivalent (i.e., just as Jewish) to the Ultra-Orthodox person whose practices may be over the top in terms of observance. Whether the first one is a "good Jew" is another question, of course. Karl Marx descended from a fine rabbinical family, but no rabbi would want him as a son-in-law. The same goes for the philosopher Spinoza who, like Marx, never denied he was Jewish but he did deny the divine origins of the Torah. In the seventeenth century, that was a good reason for his community to expel him from their midst and prevent him from having a Jewish funeral.

Someone who was not born to Jewish parents—more specifically, a Jewish mother, even if the father isn't Jewish—, is subject to the rule of religious legal authorities. The essence of Judaism is that someone who is Jewish has a Jewish soul. If this was not clear at

birth (in traditional Jewish thought the soul is placed in the body at the moment of birth) then s/he must go through some prescribed program of learning and practice of rituals to assure that one knows the fundamental teachings about Judaism and Jewish practices. Normally, these include prayers, synagogue practices, Holidays, Hebrew language, theology and history, at minimum. How, you may ask, does this assure that a Jewish soul was acquired? The answer is: it doesn't. But we have no other way of knowing this information, so it has been assumed that if one acquires generally agreed upon Jewish learning and translates it into daily practice this suffices. It may be helpful to think about this as akin to how medications are dosed. The physician looks at the patient's size, weight and age, then decides what amount of medication to start with. The problem is that we really need an indicator of liver efficiency, because this is what actually determines how rapidly or slowly the drug is metabolized. But we don't have good ways of computing liver efficiency, so we use a reasonable estimate.

As noted above, if you want to join any club, society, group, etc., you have to learn its rules and customs and stick to them. Shoshannah was born in Holland but eventually became an American citizen. She had to study many rules and facts about the government, learn about American history and society, and fill out long forms confirming that she would behave as a good citizen and obey American laws. Then, after several interviews confirming that she speaks and writes English and proving she had neither a criminal record, nor a bad past, nor bad intentions, she had to take an exam. After passing all these tests she finally got a certificate of naturalization and an American passport, on the condition that she keeps behaving in a way that qualifies her as a good citizen, who actively and constructively makes society a better place. She became a citizen out of free will and knows she has to stick to the rules. And she does. The same principles are expected from a convert who joins a Jewish community. He or she has to be an exemplary member. Otherwise, why join?

40. Are there saints in Judaism?

In Judaism, saints have an equivalent called *tzaddikim*. The world needs a certain level of justice, *tzedek* (from the same root tz-d-k) in Hebrew, which is accomplished by both the special acts of *tzaddikim* and by acts performed by everybody, such as *tzedakah*, a word that is also connected with *tzedek*. *Tzedakah* is often translated as charity. But for Jews, charity has a different meaning than the English term in general use. In the Jewish view of the world, there must be justice for everyone. To illustrate this, consider an example of giving money to a street beggar. Let's begin with the notion that the money in someone's pocket, like all money and all things in the world, belongs to G-d. It is temporarily placed in a person's pocket because of Divine Providence. On one level, we can say the beggar who has no money has an equal right to the money in someone else's pocket, because this money was placed there by G-dly forces. The person who has money in her/his pocket has a moral responsibility to share some with the beggar. And, of course, G-d is watching to see what s/he will do and keeps tabs on whether s/he does right or does wrong (we'll save a discussion about this for another time). Think of communicating vessels, the ideal situation would be that everybody gets what they need, and our "pockets" are all at the same level. Since that is not the case, the least we must do is share some of our abundance with

117

someone who is in need. In the Jewish tradition, even a beggar has to give *tzedakah* from what s/he earns (read: gets from passersby), although not a large amount, of course. The Talmud states: a *peruta*, which was the smallest coin that existed at the time must be given. By giving *tzedakah* we try to restore the balance of justice, *tzedek*. In addition, the truly observant Jew has an obligation to give money without question, because there is a need, an imbalance in the world that can easily be corrected. Giving comes from a higher sense of good that derives from a higher soul level (*neshamah*) reflecting Torah teachings. The lower levels of soul are more about self, and take the position "It's my money and I'm keeping it." This is a different way than we usually think about charitable giving, where we might listen to the beggars's story, and if we are moved by it, and only then, we will we reach into our pocket and give money. This obligation reminds us of a humorous anecdote which contains a deep truth.

Once, a town became so prosperous that there was only one beggar left. He went from house to house, but wasn't always happy with what he got. He threatened the town's people: "If you don't increase the amount you put in my hand I will leave this town! And then you are stuck, because to whom will you fulfill the obligatory *mitzvah* (divine command) to give *tzedakah*?"

We might consider the act of giving to be what a righteous person would do. We might also consider the beggar to be serving a G-dly purpose. Without the beggar the person with money in her or his pocket might not have had the opportunity to demonstrate willingness to behave in a way that brought about an act of righteousness in the world. So, who is the righteous person? Is it the person who gave the money, or is it the person who created the need for money to be given? The answer is that it could be either, or both, of these people. Without question, the one who is the selfless giver is engaging in a righteous act. But the other's purpose in life may be to give people the opportunity to test their mettle. So, if *tzedakah* is a *mitzvah* for everybody, does that make you a *tzaddik*, a saint? Not necessarily, because a *tzaddik* is one who goes above and beyond, one who fights off or overcomes temptations more than ordinary people, and does his/her utmost to—in the words of the Talmud—make G-d's will his/her will, and behaves accordingly. Moreover, a *tzaddik* often has power and knowledge of the Upper World and can guide other people to become better Jews and better human beings. In fact, we have a belief in Judaism that G-d continues to keep the world going because of the merit of thirty-six–*lamed vav* in Hebrew–hidden *tzaddikim*. This view holds that at any given point in time there are thirty-six special and very saintly people in our midst throughout the world who are going about their business under the radar, so to speak. They are often disguised as simple, unlearned, and unremarkable, but good and honest people. But of course, there are many more than those thirty-six hidden *tzaddikim*. There are also righteous people who are doing G-d's work in a public way and are quite obvious. Naturally, not all of these saintly people are Jewish, although the Hebrew word *tzaddik* is generally used for Jewish extraordinarily righteous people. Take the example of Mother Teresa. She was a Catholic nun who did missionary work with the extremely poor in India for fifty years. She was a Nobel Peace Prize laureate and was canonized by the Catholic Church as a saint. A few years ago, some curious investigative reporters found damning information on some of her unholy acts, including accepting and refusing to return stolen money, which was then used to carry out her noble works. While such news was disheartening, it doesn't diminish the significance of the good she did in the world. Most saintly people, Jews and non-Jews

alike, have a little speck or spot on their splendorous life or acts, but that does not diminish the good they do. We have an old Yiddish expression as follows: "The bigger the *tzaddik*, the bigger the *yetzer hara* (evil inclination which tempts one to behave badly)," In other words, temptation for a righteous person can be huge, but if s/he is truly righteous s/he will overcome this, with G-d's help, and help her/his fellow humans in extraordinary ways.

We need to mention one more thing here. In the non-Jewish world, saints are often associated with miracles. In Judaism we have miracles as well, to start with the biblical miracles performed by G-d, like splitting the Sea of Reeds or having the sun temporarily stop in its orbit. There are Jewish prophets and *tzaddikim* who perform miracles, always with G-d's help and as an instrument of G'd's Hand. Chassidic stories talk at length about miracle rebbes, miracle workers (*ba'alei mofet*), great and righteous people, often rabbis, who are able to beg Heaven to perform a miracle for them or those they want to help. But unlike in Christian theology, we do not call a *tzaddik* a saint because he or she is able to perform miracles. And not everybody who is able to have a miracle performed for him or her is a *tzaddik*. Another noteworthy point is that Christian saints are often famous as martyrs for their faith. There were also Jewish *tzaddikim* who were killed in horrible ways because of their faith—and their refusal to give it up—but even in such cases we stress the deeds of the living *tzaddik* rather than his death as a martyr. We call martyrs who died to defend their Jewish faith and identity *kedoshim*, "holy ones," which is the correct more accurate translation of saint (from the Latin *sanctus*, "holy"), but to be a *kadosh*, a holy one who sanctifies the Name of the Creator of the World, you don't necessarily have to be a good, moral person living a Torah lifestyle. You merely have to be killed for the sanctification of His Name, which usually happens without your consent. There are stories about thieves with a less than sterling lifestyle who in the end were killed not just because they were criminals, but because they refused to give up their Jewish identity. And they were called *kadosh*, a "holy martyr." So, are there Jewish saints like those venerated by the Catholic Church, who perform miracles, for whom altars were erected in chapels and churches, and who are asked to mediate and pray for the sinful the mortal human being and the divine Power? No. We have a completely different system. This topic is, of course, a lot more complicated than we can describe here in just a few short remarks, but a Jew always studies, so you can research more about saints and miracles yourself, or preferably with your teacher.

41.   What does sitting *shivah* mean?

A non-Jewish acquaintance of Bruce's once related a story of a time when he was young. He received a phone call from his Jewish paternal grandmother who said a relative was sitting *shivah*. Thinking they were cold and *shivering*, he offered to bring some blankets. But *Shivah* has nothing to do wit the English word shivering. It means the seven—*sheva* in Hebrew—days of mourning for parents, children, or a spouse who passed away. It has nothing to do with shivering. In Judaism, there are many rituals for dealing with a variety of life events. In fact, in a book we co-authored, we describe a series of rituals for stopping smoking (see suggested readings at the end of this book). Dealing with dying and death is something all people have to face at some time in their lives. In Judaism, we have well formulated rules for dealing with loss. When someone passes away we do not begin the mourning process until after the funeral. There is a period of intense mourning for a period of seven (*sheva*) days. The immediate family remains in a home designated for *shivah* where well-wishers come to pay their respects. Food is often brought by those desiring to assist the family in their time of grief, because mourners are not supposed to busy themselves in the kitchen or do household chores. There is a *tzedakah* (charity) box on the table. Visitors give to charity, because according to an old Talmudic story "charity saves from death." In that story a woman was saved literally from being stung by a scorpion hiding in a wall because she took time to give charity to a beggar on her wedding day when she was extremely busy. Mirrors are covered—an ancient custom from times where we believed that the spirit of the deceased might show himself in a mirror, and also as a sign that we are so immersed in grief that we don't care about our appearance, our hair, our makeup—and family members sit on uncomfortable, low-chairs, hence the expression "sitting *shivah*." Often they wear slippers or house shoes to show that they are too sad to go out. For deceased parents or children, a ritual

cut or tear was made in the lapel of an outer garment. This refers to the biblical ritual of rending one's clothes as a sign of mourning. The goal is to assure that mourning is completed by the family. One does not start talking when visiting a mourner, but waits until the mourner begins to speak. This gives the mourner a chance to tell stories about the deceased loved one, show photos, share anecdotes, or talk about something different. When one leaves, one wishes the mourner(s): "May the Almighty comfort you among the mourners of Zion and Jerusalem." A slightly less intense mourning continues for a period of 30 days, but here, the counting begins at the time of death rather than from the burial. This period is termed *Sheloshim* (which means "thirty"). Family members return to work, school and other normal activities but are not permitted to attend joyous events or participate in pleasurable activities such as visiting concerts, except for the celebration of Shabbat or religious Holidays. A daily prayer called *Kaddish* is said for the next eleven months and then on the anniversary, or *yahrzeit*, of the death. There is an image containing the text of the Kaddish in Question ,43. *Kaddish* is a prayer that includes nothing about death, instead only focuses on G-d's majesty, and requires a *minyan*, or quorum of ten Jewish people. In most Orthodox circles it includes only adult males over the *Bar Mitzvah* age of thirteen; for others, women are included. In modern times, most assimilated Jews commonly have an abridged period of *shivah* that may last only three days, in part because their boss expects them back in the workplace. In Jewish numerology, called *Gematria*, three is also significant because it signifies completion. In the case of dealing with death we lean toward support of the Jewish rituals, not because we are sticklers for following the laws. Rather, we know that when dealing with death Jewish laws have been proven to be effective for allowing mourners to achieve a more complete resolution enabling them to continue their lives. When mourning is not fully completed it can lead to psychological limitations that can last for many years. From what we've observed this is less common in the Jewish community, largely because of our defined mourning rituals which allow us to work through our grief. Preferably one does not grieve alone, but rather with his or her community. It is a *mitzvah* and a great kindness (*chesed*) to visit someone who is mourning, even if you know them only superficially from, for instance, the synagogue or a shop.

42. Do Jews believe in an afterlife?

Yes, we do. This is not an easy topic to discuss, because there are differing opinions about what happens to the soul after death. Personally, we prefer the traditional mystical view. In this view, the soul has five levels. The lower levels are associated with the body. The higher levels of spirituality are associated with the non-corporeal aspects of life and ascend after the physical body is no longer operational. The soul ascends to "The place where souls go," as it has been described, which is commonly referred to as "Heaven." In mystical writings it is said that some souls remain there until they are ready to be placed into another body, so they can have another chance to become further refined spiritually. When the soul becomes sufficiently purified through making good choices about life experiences it gains entry to Paradise. This is the Jewish notion of the transmigration of souls. We prefer this to the explanation that when we die we simply cease to exist and our bodies deteriorate and become food for the worms. While this may be a simple explanation, it flies in the face of the conception of Jewish spirituality, because it denies the existence of the soul, which in Jewish theology is essential to explaining human existence and our relationship with the Almighty.

It says in Proverbs (2:27) that the human spirit, or soul, is the lamp of G-d. Would G-d let His lamp be extinguished and disappear? Rather, the divine spark in every human soul will be reunited with its divine source. According to our tradition, every Jew was present at Mount Sinai to receive and accept the Torah (Deuteronomy 29:14). Some were in bodies and some were not. We believe that all Jews, those from the past and those living now, are these souls. But aren't there many more people around nowadays than there were then? This can be compared to the flame of a candle which can divide itself into many other flames while staying the same flame. Souls, likewise, occupy a body and return after that body dies to their divine origin, the "original flame." In case they need to be cleansed from sin they may stay around for another few cycles in this world, in different bodies. In Judaism, the soul is immortal and eternal. It waits for the resurrection of the dead in Messianic times. At that time it will be reunited with its restored bodily garment in a better world. As with many subjects brought up in the questions in our book, we must say that volumes have been written about these issues and we cannot explain everything in a few sentences. We encourage you to research this subject with your study partner, rabbi, or online because this one is truly fascinating.

43. If I have a tattoo, can I be buried in a Jewish cemetery?

Yes. There is a myth that has been going around for decades that if a Jew has a tattoo s/he is not permitted to be buried in a Jewish cemetery or have a Jewish funeral. During the Holocaust, many Jews were tattooed with numbers for identification, much against their will. They have been buried in Jewish cemeteries in the event they survived the war. But we do have a prohibition against tattooing our bodies voluntarily (Leviticus 19:28). This prohibition is derived from two sources.

First, we follow the principle that our bodies are likened to being temples that honor our Creator. Our bodies, like our souls, do not really belong to us. They belong to our Creator. They have been given to us for care-taking. We are judged in the Heavenly Court by how well we take care of what we've been given for safeguarding and how we live our lives. Consequently, it is considered improper to deface our bodies. But if we did, it will not prevent us from getting either a Jewish funeral or burial in a Jewish cemetery.

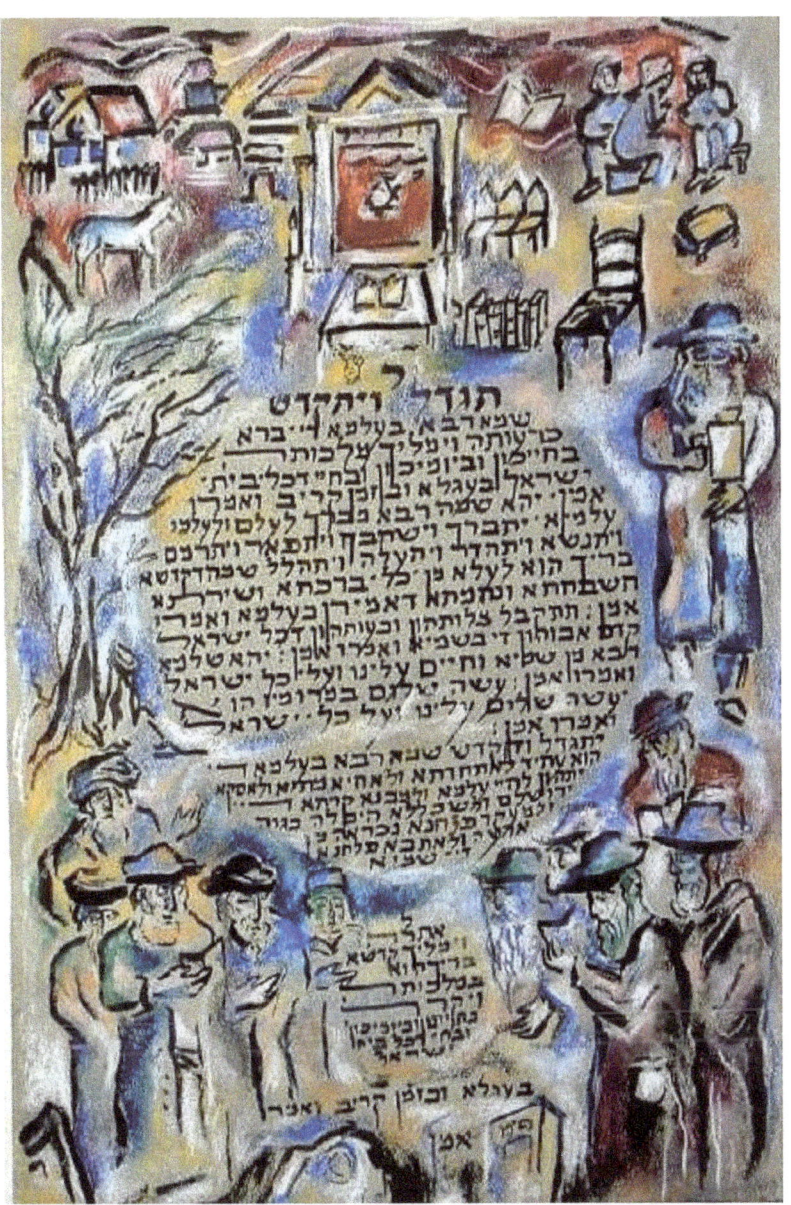

Second, in ancient times tattoos, piercings, and body scarring were practices of idolators, which Jews are strictly forbidden to emulate. Jews were enjoined from following any practices that appeared to be like those of idol worshipers out of concern that someone seeing a Jew with such body markings might think the Jew was an idol worshiper or that the practices were permissible. This is similar to the ruling made by early rabbis that since poultry looked like meat from cattle, sheep or goats, eating it with dairy products should be prohibited, so that no one could conclude a Jew was eating a forbidden combination of meat with dairy. This is the principle of *mar'it ayin*, "that what meets the eye." There is a *midrash*, a story commenting on the Torah, about a man who—understandably—wanted to hide his Jewish identity during a time of Roman persecutions. Therefore he dressed like a Roman. He entered an inn and knew that the innkeeper, secretly a pious Jew, would secretly serve *kosher* meat to any customers he knew or suspected to be Jewish. The innkeeper carefully observed who washed their hands in a certain way before eating bread, a custom that is mandatory for Jews but not observed by Romans. But the disguised Jew was lax with this custom and the innkeeper, thinking he was a non-Jew, served him non-*kosher* meat. When the customer found out, he was greatly distressed but could not blame the innkeeper; he looked like a heathen and showed no outward or secret signs of being Jewish at all, therefore he was treated like a heathen.

But what about piercing your ears to wear earrings? This is allowed and not considered defacing or damaging the body as it is done for the purpose of enhancing beauty rather than as an idolatrous practice. It is mentioned in the Torah as a normal beauty routine. Women also wore nose-rings at the time (see Ezekiel 16:11, Exodus 35:22 and other texts). There is nothing wrong with embellishing one's body with jewelry—even piercing one's ears for that purpose—or nice but modest clothes, make-up, and hair-dye, depending on what is fashionable in one's community. It is a praiseworthy custom to wear one's best jewelry on Shabbat and for a wife to beautify herself for her husband. But not with tattoos.

Along a similar vein, cremation is also prohibited. The traditional explanation is that when Moshiach, the messiah, comes all the dead will be resurrected and there will be eternal peace until the end of days. To assure that one's body can be brought back to life it is essential that all body parts, including blood, since it is considered the life force, be buried with the body so they are available when the time comes. If the body was reduced to ashes through cremation it cannot be resurrected. The only exception is if a body part was donated to save a life. In Judaism it is permitted, in fact it is required, to break commandments to save a life. This is the principle of *Pikuach Nefesh*. Cremated remains are not permitted in Jewish cemeteries and most rabbis will not officiate at a funeral in which the deceased was cremated voluntarily. Bruce once officiated at the funeral of his wife's financial planning client. The woman requested he do this during her lengthy bout with cancer. The proviso was that the woman was not Jewish and the funeral was at a non-denominational cemetery. It's a difficult question that rabbis face when a Holocaust survivor asks to be cremated after death, since their whole family was murdered and "went up the chimney." The rabbi will try to persuade the person to opt for a burial instead and even offer financial assistance if a poor person wants to be cremated for lack of money, because cremation is cheaper than buying a cemetery plot. In Israel cremation was forbidden for the longest time, but since 2007 there is a crematorium used by non-religious people. And what about the remains of people who could not be buried in one piece due to external circumstances? Think of victims of terrorist attacks who were blown up, people who die in a fire, in the Holocaust, or who drowned at sea or were devoured by animals? That is beyond their fault. They will be part of the resurrection. But we should not be cremated voluntarily by members of our family.

44. What is the Jewish belief about forgiveness?

Forgiveness is always available and in Judaism we take this very seriously. When we sin against G-d, we ask G-d for forgiveness. This occurs during many prayers, like the daily morning prayers, and it's the specific theme of the High Holy Days, Rosh Hashanah and Yom Kippur. During the time before the destruction of the Temple in Jerusalem it was the *Kohen HaGadol*, the High Priest, who was the only one permitted to enter the Holy of Holies, the inner sanctum, to confess and ask forgiveness on behalf of the entire community on Yom Kippur. Today, since we no longer have the Temple, nor do we have Temple priests,

(instead we have rabbis and cantors), we pray collectively and ask for forgiveness for all sins that may have been done by any Jew anywhere. But G-d does not forgive sins we committed against another human being unless we ask that person for forgiveness. We are obligated to ask up to three times. If the other does not grant forgiveness by then there is no need to continue. If the person we sinned against is absent, dead, or otherwise cannot be reached, the sin can't be forgiven and we live with it, trying to compensate by doing good deeds. We cannot forgive on behalf of other people. When the German chancellor Willy Brandt asked for forgiveness for the crimes perpetrated in the Third Reich of Nazi Germany, rabbis answered him that they highly appreciated the gesture, but Brandt himself had not committed the crimes, and the rabbis themselves therefore could not forgive on behalf of the victims unless they had been personally victimized. They could only forgive crimes committed against themselves. This shows us what a complicated matter crime, punishment, and forgiveness represent.

In order to receive forgiveness, we must first acknowledge wrong-doing and recognize the wrong headedness of our ways. Then we express regret and try to learn from our errors making serious efforts not to repeat the offense. We may do penance by giving to charity, performing charitable acts, prayers, and increasing our level of observance or doing good deeds.

45. Do Jews believe the Bible (Torah) is literally true?

There are Jews who believe the teachings set out in the Torah are G-d's words and are literally true. These are the Ultra-Orthodox and many Orthodox. While most Jews believe there are universal truths and lessons for living ethical and meaningful lives that are derived from Torah teachings, we tend to shy away from looking at these writings as (scientific) facts. Our opinion is that statements like "G-d created the world in six days" is literally true, if by six days we actually mean approximately 13.9 billion years divided in certain eras, like the era of vegetation only, the era of animals, etc. Who's to say that in ancient times a day meant twenty-four hours? We know that many time systems differed from the one we use now. Or that in the time of the great flood when we are told it rained for forty days and forty nights it was exactly that amount of time. We know that in those times forty was used metaphorically to indicate a large amount. It's not much different from telling a friend we can't get together because we have a million things to do. We do not mean we have precisely that many tasks. We just mean we have a lot to do. Scholars, like Steven

Weitzman at the University of Pennsylvania (cf., *The Origin of the Jews: The Quest for Roots in a Rootless Age*) emphasize Torah stories as falling within the genre of myths that embody core values and beliefs. This perspective does not diminish the value of the lessons for ethical living, but does call into question the empirical nature of certain biblical accounts. That is, they are more truths than facts. Many rabbis—among whom the famous medieval philosopher Maimonides, aka Rambam—state that the person who does believe that all the stories in the Torah, the Talmud and the commentaries must be taken literally is a fool. But he who doesn't study them intensively is a bigger fool.

Our sages taught that to make sense out of any Torah writings we must understand them on four levels. We use an acronym as a mnemonic device to remember the four methods of understanding biblical writings: PaRDeS. The first is Peshat, meaning the "literal level of understanding." Next is Remez, meaning "hints," which is explaining one biblical verse with the help of other verses and with symbolic or allegorical interpretations. Then we have Derash, which means "to inquire," referring to the homiletic or *midrashic* level of meaning. Finally, we have Sod, meaning "secret," which is the mystical or esoteric level of interpretation. In Judaism, we thus have the belief that to arrive at a fuller meaning of biblical teachings we must go beyond the literal. We also conclude that even if scriptural writings are not scientifically true or historically accurate in our modern eyes, it does not take away from life lessons, insights about human beings, or directions for living ethically that may be gleaned from studying Torah. This is one of the points of understanding we get from highly educated physical and life scientists who are also observant, religious Jews. We note the word observant. For a Jew it's much more important to perform the *mitzvot*, the commandments that we have to follow in order to live an ethical life and that govern our behavior towards G-d, our fellow humans, and society, than to believe in dogmas. There are 613 *mitzvot*. But the dogmas, the tenets of Judaism, can be told in only Thirteen Articles of Faith as stated in Question #3.

46.   Why don't Jews believe in Jesus?

We do. We just don't believe that he was the Messiah, otherwise known as Moshiach. We understand that the historical Jesus was a Jewish teacher who lived in Israel during the time of the second Temple. He was considered dangerous for the Jews in the sense that he antagonized the Romans, who were in charge at the time, with his talk about a Kingdom of G-d. The Roman authorities wondered that perhaps Jesus was planning to replace the Roman Empire with his "kingdom." There had been many insurgences against Hellenists and Romans before, usually with disastrous results for the Jews and the loss of many lives. Therefore, people like Jesus endangered the whole city of Jerusalem and the whole Jewish province of the Roman Empire, which Israel was at the time. This, in addition to persecutions in later ages by his followers, the Christians, have not earned Jesus a sweet reputation in Jewish history, even though—or despite the fact that—he himself was a Jew with a very Jewish approach in his teachings. The Muslims believed him to be a prophet but we don't, because he does not meet the standards set for Jewish prophecy. Neither can he be the Messiah, because the biblical prophecies contain a number of elements that were to happen when the Messiah comes at the end of times. These include the acceptance of the one true G-d and peace among all human beings. This was and is not the case, neither in Jesus' time nor any time thereafter including the present, and consequently there is continued dispute over Jesus being the Messiah. Jews believe he was not, which for Christians has been a reason for harsh persecutions until not so long ago. Over the course of Jewish history there have been a number of people thought to be Messiah. The most recent one was the late Lubavitcher Rebbe Menachem Mendel Schneerson (1902-1994). He, too, has been discredited for exactly the same reason as all of the other previous false Messiahs. But that hasn't dissuaded those who continue to have this belief, which might be summed up in the statement: "Don't try to confuse me with facts. My mind is made up." Although Christianity is totally rooted in Judaism, and Jesus and his followers were religious Jews, it has developed into a completely different religion with its own unique tenets. And one of these tenets is the divinity of Jesus the Messiah, who is the son of G-d, which Jews patently reject. Some may ask why the Jews don't write more about Jesus from a Jewish point of view? Although there are studies about Jesus written by Jews we simply have other, more significant people to write about, like prophets and scholars we follow, to begin with Moses.

47. Why does the Sabbath fall on Saturday instead of Sunday?

According to the Torah, in the first chapter of Genesis, G-d spoke and created the world on a Sunday, and completed His work on Friday when human beings came into existence. Then He rested from creating and stopped on Saturday, *Shabbat*, which comes from the root *sh-v-t*, to rest or cease. Unlike days in the general accepted system in our society, Jewish days begin the evening before, after dark. This means that the creation of the world stopped on Friday evening before dark. From Friday evening until Saturday evening after dark there is a period of rest and abstinence from work, called Shabbat. Today, even on Gregorian weekly or monthly calendars currently in use we see weeks as starting on Sunday.

A more interesting question then becomes: Why do Christians observe the "Sabbath" on Sunday? The early Christians were Jews. In fact, at the very beginning the only ones who were accepted by the newly established Christian sect and brought into the fold were Jews. But there are some historical and theological reasons why Christians moved Sabbath observance to Sunday. The early Christians noted that Saturday was a day of rest created by G-d for humans to emulate Him, ceasing all work and dedicating themselves to worship. This is based on Genesis 2: 2,3. But later on, non-Jews joined the growing group of Christians. In several places in the Christian Bible, or New Testament, it was stated that they were exempt from following laws contained in the Jewish Bible, the Torah, (e.g., Romans 7:1-4). They also noted that Christ's resurrection occurred on the first day of the week, Sunday, and there was a custom followed by early Christians to meet for religious assembly on Sundays. Eventually, Christians adopted Sundays as their Sabbath and it became formalized within religious practice, amongst others to distinguish between them and the Jews who only follow the "Old Testament," observe Shabbat on the seventh day, as stated in the Torah, and do not accept the doctrine of Jesus the Messiah and his resurrection. It is interesting that not only the Christians claim that the laws of the Torah must be observed solely by Jews, as Jesus commanded in Mathew 5:17-48, but Jews claim that non-Jews are only obligated to observe the so-called seven Noahide Laws, which basically demand moral behavior, and not the Torah with its 613 complicated precepts.

The Noahide Laws include proclaiming that God is one, not committing idolatry, not cursing Him or His name, not committing murder, not eating meat cut form an animal that is still alive, a practice that existed in times when refrigerating meat was not possible and cutting it from a live animal ensured freshness, but caused pain and anguish to the poor animal, not stealing, decent sexual behavior, and setting up courts of law in order to promote a just society.

All these laws apply to Jews and non-Jews alike. But eating kosher, observing Shabbat and Yom Tov, and a myriad of other (complicated) laws, several of which were tied to the Temple in Jerusalem, only apply to Jews. Those converting to Judaism don't make it easy for themselves by accepting so many more *mitzvot*.

48.   Do I have to grow a beard? Must I cover my hair?

According to a rabbinic interpretation of the text contained in Leviticus 19:27, shaving with a razor is prohibited. An electric shaver or scissors have been deemed acceptable according to some interpretations. The prohibition is considered to be part of Jewish law, which is termed *Halakhah*. Outside of Orthodox and Ultra-Orthodox circles shaving of facial hair is considered optional. So, it's up to you, as it is not required. Like most decisions in Judaism, what is done should reflect your level of observance and your community. But if you are leaning toward traditional observance you may want to look more closely at the laws about shaving body hair. There are different rules for men than for women. For example, men should not "manscape" since they would be doing what women do, and that is a no-no. Women may trim the hair in armpits and pubic areas. Men are prohibited from doing the same, because it is (or at least was) not a male custom. This comes by extension of the law prohibiting men and women from wearing each other's clothing. What men and women can do or should (not) do with their bodies and clothing is complicated and based on several Torah rules which have been explained at length in the Talmud and commentaries, but these rules are also subject to subtle (social) changes in different times and communities. For instance, women wearing pants is normal in some modern communities and frowned upon in some-but not all-more traditional or very Orthodox communities. And now that we are talking about hair, in most Ashkenazy Jewish communities men cover their head with a *kippah*, or *yarmulke*, a small round skullcap, the word being derived from *yerei elo-him*, G-d fearing, respecting G-d. It is a sign that there is Somebody, a Higher Power, above you. But few religious Sephardic men wear a *kippah* in public, choosing instead to don it in the synagogue, which is acceptable in their community. In New York, some Orthodox Jewish lawyers wear a *yarmulke* at all times, but in most communities they do not, because it is against the dress-code of their profession. Many Orthodox men wear a head-covering, like a hat, baseball cap, or *yarmulke* all the time. Some don't. Every community has their own standards. For women there are social rules as well. According to the Talmud, a married woman must cover her hair. In many Orthodox circles married women cover their hair with a scarf (called *tichel* in Yiddish), hat, beret, or a wig (*shaytel* in Yiddish) out of modesty. The hair of a woman, especially when it is long and beautiful, has been associated with strong mystical powers, it is sexually enticing, and should be seen only by a woman's husband at home but not by other men. Some rabbis in Ultra-Orthodox circles object to a wig, because it is often prettier than a woman's own hair, not to mention the lack of bad hair days, and it might attract undue male attention. Other rabbis, like Chabad chassidim, explicitly prescribe a wig, to make a woman feel pretty and comfortable in our modern society. But her real hair, which is considered part of her real beauty, is reserved for her husband and hidden in public. A covered head shows that the woman in question is married, just like a wedding ring. But covering her hair isn't the custom in non-Orthodox circles and among most modern Orthodox women in the US, who can choose whether they cover their hair only in the synagogue, a little bit, or not at all. The same applies to dress style in different communities; in some women wear only long skirts and long sleeves, in others they don't. To explain all the differences requires a lengthy discussion. When you convert you usually look at the standards in your community and stick with them.

49. Does "Jew radar" really exist?

We've never heard of any research on the subject, but we have experienced this phenomenon ourselves. And when we check this out with other Jews we get confirmation that it is real. In fact, if you were to say the term "Jew radar" to other American Jews, most of the time they know exactly what you're talking about. In the world of behavioral science, this is known as consensual validation. But in actuality this is probably just confirmation bias. Shoshannah, who was born in Amsterdam, spots average Dutch people in the subway in Brooklyn right away, and not because she hears them speaking Dutch. They would not spot her; however, because she is too short, not blond, and looks different from the average Dutch person. Not only physically, but her behavior is different as well. So, does "Dutch radar" also exist? If we talk with others who have similar cultural experiences when we talk about certain values or life experiences we are likely to find agreement. When this happens, we get a positive feeling and associate this with being Jewish. But if it were real, it would happen when a Jew from Thailand and a Jew from the Middle East meet, Yes, there are Jews in Thailand and other Asian countries; but not Malaysia, one of the most antisemitic and corrupt countries in the world. Jew radar does not work in most cases. So, while we might have a nice feeling of being connected to other Jews, and even view them in a more positive light than non-Jews, this does not provide the empirical validation we would need to validate the existence of Jew radar. We have to conclude that Jew radar has no scientific basis and does not truly exist. And sometimes it backfires on those who insist it exists. Shoshannah was at a Jewish wedding where one of the guests was a non-Jewish Italian-American whose grandparents came from Italy. Most people were convinced that he was Sephardic. But he was not. There is an old joke about an American, Orthodox, Ashkenazy, typically "Jewish looking" businessman from New York who visits a remote Chinese provincial town. He didn't think that there are Jews in that town. There isn't even a Chabad house, a little *shul* and hospitality center of Chabad Chassidim which can be found in many distant places on the planet. On Friday evening, he feels a bit lonely in his hotel and decides to go for a Shabbos walk. He gets lost and ends up in a little street. All of a sudden, he hears singing the Shabbos hymn *lekha dodi* welcoming "Bride Shabbat" behind a wall. Here? In China? Is he imagining it? He has to check that out! He finds an entrance gate in the wall. Behind it is a *shul*, complete with

an *Aron Kodesh* (shrine for the Torah scrolls), and men and women *davening* (praying) in Hebrew. However, they all look Chinese. Befuddled but happy, he grabs a prayer book and joins the Service. Afterwards the rabbi comes to greet him. The rabbi has *payos* (traditional side-locks) and a *yarmulke* (a skullcap), but he also wears a silk Chinese gown and has a very Chinese face, just like all the other congregants. "Welcome sir, Shabbat shalom, I saw you come in and join our Service. Pardon me for asking, but are you perhaps Jewish?" The businessman with the very Jewish face (according to western standards, that is) affirms this, "I am Avrum Goldstein from Brooklyn, New York, and I am Jewish indeed." The Chinese rabbi shakes his head. "Funny, you don't look Jewish."

No matter what people say or don't say, if you have converted you are as Jewish as anybody else and it is not important where or in what religion your ancestors were born and how you look.

50.   Once I finish conversion do I have to do anything else?

Do you remember when you finished high school and you were told a commencement ceremony would be held to commemorate graduation? It seemed like an odd word to use, because you were finished with school, since commencement means beginning. Once you finish the conversion, it means that from that day forward you go through life as a Jew. This is a new beginning. Nothing else is required of you except to come to an understanding of what it means to be Jewish. Judaism reveres learning, especially Torah learning, and acting, especially doing *mitzvot*. We hear it said that more than Jewish people kept the Torah alive, the Torah kept the Jewish people alive. Like we mentioned earlier, there is a *midrash*, a religious inspiring story, that tells us that *Moshiach*'s donkey is a metaphor for the Torah, because it "carried" and supported us through our Exile and it will ultimately carry Moshiach on its back to bring the Redemption. An appreciation for life-long learning, especially about Jewish ethics, laws, interpretations, customs, and practices is what is expected of you, as well as moral standards and behavior in accordance with the Torah and its explications. It doesn't have to happen all at once, but for a Jew, learning and refining themselves perpetually are a *conditio sine qua non.* Perhaps each year, during the High Holy Days, you can decide to take on one or more new *mitzvot*, or a new text to study, or a new practice. Or, you can assume more responsibilities quickly. Each thing you do increases your consciousness of the Almighty, elevates you spiritually, and brings you closer to G-d. It is a journey in which you become a better human being. It never ends. We see this embodied in the Jewish custom to leave one wall inside the home unfinished—for instance, by leaving a little square unpainted or not plastered —so that we are reminded that the Temple has been destroyed, the world is broken and not a harmonious place, each of us is a work in progress, as is the world, and each of us is obligated to do our part to make improvements in the world. This is known as *tikkun olam (repairing the world)* and is an important Jewish principle. We are partners with G-d to improve the world. We start with ourselves. But how?
Go out and learn! For a Jew, learning never stops.

Concluding Comments on the Future of Judaism

If you were planning on buying a new car it would be a good idea to do a little research to make sure it will last a few years. Similarly, if you were considering investing in a business or joining an exclusive country club you'd certainly want to conduct some due diligence, so you have assurance that they would thrive and still be in operation in the future, so that your investment is secure. The same goes for Judaism. If you are thinking of converting to Judaism it is wise to have some concerns about the future. We'd like to share our ideas with you.

In ancient Rome, Circus Maximus was host to as many as 150,000 spectators. They reveled in events such as chariot races, gladiators who fought to their deaths, and even public executions. These were all considered fitting forms of entertainment reflecting social values and customs. In 1871, the Ringling Brothers of Wisconsin started their circus. Nearly fifty years later, they merged with the Barnum and Bailey Circus to form what was billed as "The Greatest Show on Earth," as it was one of the largest entertainment empires in the US. It was born of Victorian era values emphasizing Eurocentric supremacy and racism. Their shows included not only clowns, high wire acts and people being shot out of cannons, but also had numerous animal acts and "freak shows," showcasing dwarves, bearded women, people with various genetic mutations, and "exotic people" from Africa or Asia on display like wild animals. For decades there was broad acceptance of laughing and gawking at those with physical anomalies or of different appearance, and abuse of animals. Eventually, the norms of civility changed, and in May 2017 Ringling Brothers and Barnum & Bailey Circus shut their doors. In days gone by, we accepted and even enjoyed the spectacles. But in time there was a groundswell of outrage, as social norms change in the same way styles of protective garments and fashion do. Today, Cirque du Soleil, the world's largest theatrical producer, combines theatrics, acrobats, and music into high tech shows that captivate audiences. The popularity of these shows are part of the changing fabric of sensibilities and what defines good taste. We believe the same is true of Judaism, despite the views of those who would have us cling to the past. While Shoshannah and Bruce cherish our European and Chassidic heritage we are puzzled by mindless adherence to such customs as assuming the dress of eighteenth century Polish nobility often seen among our co-religionists. For instance, wearing Chassidic fur hats, *shtraymels,* make sense in cold Polish winters but in hot Brooklyn or Israeli summers, and one wonders if it's not better—and healthier—to adopt lighter headwear. Further, we question the need to blindly follow some aspects of our tradition, especially in the face of evolving social norms and scientifically derived knowledge (e.g., evolution and global warming) and we believe that if Judaism is to survive and flourish we must make sensible modifications to our practices that reflect a changing world. This idea is not new. The medieval scholar and philosopher Moses Maimonides promoted this train of thought. And he is not the only one in Jewish history.

A small example of how things are changing is the Orthodox ritual of *kapoyrah shlugn* before Yom Kippur. It has no roots in the Torah and, in fact, its origins are pretty obscure. This ritual begins by saying several blessings, then one's sins are symbolically transferred to a living hen or rooster which one swings over one's head and the heads of one's family. Then, the animal is slaughtered and given to the poor, so they have meat for the next Shabbat or Holiday on their table. In ancient societies, it was not common for poor people to have meat or poultry on a regular basis. In a rural society, where people know how to handle animals, the chicken was gently swung once and then slaughtered. In Brooklyn, however, chickens are kept in crates in parking lots, rain and shine, and swung several times by different city people who have no idea how to hold on to a chicken and may hurt it. Many rabbis say that you can substitute the chicken with a (dead) fish or, even better, with money, which is given to the poor afterwards. That is a lot kinder for both animals and people. Although some traditionalists might balk at this change, more and more Jews now use money when they perform *kapoyrah shlugn*. So do we, change with the times and hopefully our children will only know the ritual with the live chicken from old paintings in books, or from Shoshannah's drawings. An important Jewish principle is to be humane and compassionate, and to diminish or end suffering, and to make people, animals, in short, to make the world the best and healthiest place you can. We spoke earlier about *tikkun olam* (improving/healing the world). Does that imply, for instance, that we all have to become vegetarians, as many modern Jews do? Not necessarily. Our ancestors were nomads and farmers. They kept animals and had herds. They ate meat and sacrificed animals of their flocks to honor G-d in the Temple in Jerusalem. According to the Torah, we are allowed to eat meat, but only on condition that we minimize stress and suffering of the animal. There are strict rules about ritual slaughter, like the sharpness of the *shochet's* (trained ritual butchers) knife, the swiftness of the cut and the quick loss of consciousness by bleeding the animal. If it is not slaughtered the right (read: most humane) way it is rendered *trayfe,* i.e., not *kosher* and therefore unfit for consumption by observant Jews. Non-Jews don't have to observe the strict laws of *shechitah* (ritual slaughter), although it is praiseworthy, of course, to slaughter animals in the least painful way. But the seven universal Noahide laws for all mankind forbid eating meat that has been cut from a living animal, which seems to have been practiced in the hot Middle-eastern climate in order to make sure the "dead" meat wasn't spoiled. But the animal suffered tremendously. And that is forbidden in Judaism. Not slaughtering animals at all diminishes suffering even more. Our ancestors lacked the knowledge about climate change and pollution we have and therefore some people living now give up eating meat altogether. It's their choice.

As noted in Question #6, we are concerned about the future of Jewry and the potential damage caused by insufficient variety in the gene pool. As much as we'd like to see Jews marrying other Jews, Bruce wants to extend this observation, and in fact, advocate for conversion. According to a Pew Research Center study, 40% of all newly married people in the US are of different faiths. Among Jews, the intermarriage rate is nearly 60%. We are not saying here that this is either good or bad, although intermarried couples are less likely to have a Jewish home or raise Jewish children. These are simply the facts. As it now stands, due to differing birth rates future Jews appear more likely to be Ultra-Orthodox. This group tends to have a high birth rate. Not only compared with non-Orthodox Jews, but in contrast to the general population as well. Chassidic Jews are insular and marry within their own group. While this may have been important at one time in history, given the large number of genetic disorders found among Jews, this is no longer the case. Less diversity in the gene pool puts a greater number of Jews at risk for developing afflictions such as Tay-Sachs, Kreutzfeldt-Jakob, and Gaucher's disease, to name a few. Rather than assuring the survival of Jews and traditional Judaism it makes both more likely to face extinction. In Israel, Jews from all over the world meet and mingle, and it's actually beneficial for Middle-eastern, like Iraqi, Jews to marry Ashkenazy women with ancestors from Western Europe, or for a Spanish-Sephardic bride to choose a Russian Jewish husband.

We anticipate that in the future Jewish perspectives will be considered within an evolving social context. For example, currently there is concern about a woman's right to choose for abortion and how the Supreme Court of the United States will address this complex issue. There are differing perspectives on when life begins and, therefore, how a just society should address the matter. Ideally, it should be grounded in constitutional ideals and the law and not be influenced by morality derived from faith traditions. Yet, it is not black and white, and no matter which side of the issue one takes, there are theological underpinnings. The Christian notion is that life begins at conception. By contrast, the Jewish view is that while all life is holy and should be protected, life begins at the moment of birth, because this is when a soul is acquired. A fetus younger than 40 days is not considered a person yet and abortion of such a fetus is viewed differently than the abortion of an older fetus. To cause a woman to miscarry is not punished as murder but as causing damage according to the Jewish law. The rules are very complex and we can't go into that here.

There is also the issue of how we should address immigration. For Jews, we have the biblical injunction to treat outsiders with kindness since we were once "strangers in the land of Egypt." Many Jews are involved in organizations helping immigrants, illegals, and refugees. It's part of our history and in our genes.

Finally, we are hopeful that as civilization advances we will see wider acceptance, perhaps even celebration, of diversity that embraces cultural, ethnic, racial, religious and gender identity differences. And that the Jewish perspective that emphasizes higher levels of spirituality's association with social justice will find broader acceptance particularly in regard to the Middle East.

In many, if not most, organizations advocating social justice Jews are represented in large numbers, often much larger than our proportional representation of the population at large. American Jews marched with Black people who were denied equality and racial justice. Rabbi Abraham Joshua Heschel accompanied Rev. Martin Luther King on the famous march from Selma to Montgomery. In the spring of 2020 a Black man, George Floyd, was killed as the result of racial police violence. Many Jews joined the Black protest and held vigils. Even the Orthodox community in Brooklyn, which usually doesn't engage in political protests, organized events and a march. With our long history and our ethical guidance of the Torah we follow the dictum "Justice, Justice shall you pursue" (Deuteronomy 16:20). But what is justice? Having studied the Talmud and scriptures diligently for millennia, we have sharpened our minds and hearts to investigate and discuss this.

By now it should be evident that being a Jew is extremely difficult because, aside from dealing with a variety of negative if not blatantly hostile forces, it means that one is always questioning, always asking oneself what is right, what is moral, and what is just, rather than what is convenient and comfortable. To study and to question, that is what defines a Jew, and we would like to see all Jews—whether Jewish by birth or by conversion—incorporate this practice into their lives.

Other works by the authors:

- **Brombacher, S., Hamburger, H.**: *I See Only Light*
- **Schwartz, R., Brombacher, S.**: *Holy Eating*
- **Brombacher, S., Buxbaum, Y.**: *Serach, a Seder Companion*
- **Forman, B., Brombacher, S.**: *Under the Chuppah, A Jewish Couple's Guide to Weddings and Meaningful Marriage*
- **Brombacher, S.**: *Painting the Dybbuk. Between Two Worlds. Ansky's Play seen through an Artist's Lens*
- **Brombacher, S.**: *The Little Rose on the Mountain*
- **Forman, B., Brombacher, S.**: *Smokescreen: A Jewish Approach to Stop Smoking*
- **Brombacher, S.**: *The Golem in Brooklyn: The Golem Exhibition at the Brooklyn Jewish Art gallery at CKI*
- **Seidman, R., Brombacher, S.**: *A New Oracle of Kabbalah: Mystical Teachings of the Hebrew Letters: For Insight, Perspective, and Guidance*
- **Brombacher, S., Zaklikowsky, D.**: *On One Foot. The Life of Hillel*
- **Brombacher, S.**: *Pictorial for The Story of My Life. Various Events and Episodes of an Orphan By Pinkhes-Dov Goldenshteyn: Seen through the eyes of an artist*
- **Brombacher, S.**: *Haggadah shel Pesach / - The Passover Hagadah*
- **Brombacher, S.**: *For Strangers passing Through* (Illustrated Chassidic stories)
- **Forman, B., Kaplan, S., Brombacher, S.**: *Rebbe Nachman's Tales: Stories for Personal Refinement*
- **Dalfin, Ch., Brombacher, S., et al. ed. Chava Witkes**: *Inspired. Rosh Hashanah Prayer Companion*
- **Forman, B., Forman, K..**: *Fundamentals of Marketing the Private Psychotherapy Practice*
- **Forman, B., Silverman, W..**: *Answers to the 50 Most Important Questions About Private Mental Health Practice*
- **Kaplan, S., Forman, B.**: *Clinical Pastoral Psychotherapy: Perspectives and Methods*

SUGGESTED READING:

Barnavi, E. (Ed.): A Historical Atlas of the Jewish People (2002) **Buber, M.:** Tales of the Hasidim (1991)

Buber, M.: On Judaism (1996)

Buxbaum, Y.: Jewish Spiritual Practices (1999) Donin, H.: *To Pray as a Jew* (1980)

Gersh, H.: *When a Jew Celebrates* (1971)

Greenberg, B.: *How to Run a Traditional Jewish Household* (1985)

Greene, C. F.: *Almost Jewish: Converting to Judaism the Hard Way* (2017)

Heschel, A.: *A Passion for Truth* (1995)

Kitov, E.: *The Book of Our Heritage* (1973)

Maimonides, M. (translated by Friedlander, M.): *Guide for the Perplexed* (2018, many editions available)

Stein, P.: *Jews for Joy: An Enlightening Novel* (2019)

Telushkin, J.: *Jewish Literacy* (2001)

Telushkin, J.: *A code of Jewish ethic, Vol. 1: You shall be holy* (2006)

Wagner, J.L.: *The Synagogue Survival Kit* (1997)

Wolpe, D.: *Why Faith Matters* (2009)

Internet resources for learning:

    http://www.GoldharSchool.com
    http://www.BimBam.com
    http://www.chabad.org

About the art in this book:

Most of the art in this book is for sale. For more information contact artist Shoshannah Brombacher.

e-mail: shoshbm@gmail.com
Website: www.absolutearts.com/s/portfolios/shoshannah
Facebook or **academia.edu**: Shoshannah Brombacher

About the Authors:

Shoshannah Brombacher received her PhD in Jewish Studies from the University of Leiden (Holland), lectured and researched in Berlin and Jerusalem, and is well-known in the Jewish art world. She participated in and curated many exhibitions. She is also an ordained maggidah (i.e., spiritual teacher and storyteller) and has published numerous stories (see www.chabad.org), contributed numerous articles to a variety of lay and scholarly publications, has done cover art and illustrations for a number of authors, including Yitzhak Buxbaum, and has authored several books of her own. After many years in Brooklyn she currently resides in Berlin (Germany). Brombacher is the vice-president of the American Guild of Judaic Art.

Bruce D. Forman holds a PhD from Duke University. He also holds ordination as both a rabbi and a maggid. Formerly an academic, he now practices psychology in South Florida in addition to serving the unaffiliated Jewish community. He has authored/co-authored seven books and over sixty scientific and professional articles and book chapters.

Now go out and learn.

www.ingramcontent.com/pod-product-compliance
Lightning Source LLC
Chambersburg PA
CBHW040042100526
44583CB00027BA/3256